Qualitative Marketing Research

Qualitative Marketing Research

Understanding How Behavioral Complexities Drive Marketing Strategies

Rajagopal

BEP BUSINESS EXPERT PRESS

Qualitative Marketing Research: Understanding How Behavioral Complexities Drive Marketing Strategies

Copyright © Business Expert Press, LLC, 2019.

First published in 2019 by
Business Expert Press, LLC
222 East 46th Street, New York, NY 10017
www.businessexpertpress.com

ISBN-13: 978-1-94999-101-7 (paperback)
ISBN-13: 978-1-94999-102-4 (e-book)

Business Expert Press Marketing Collection

Collection ISSN: 2150-9654 (print)
Collection ISSN: 2150-9662 (electronic)

Cover and interior design by Exeter Premedia Services Private Ltd., Chennai, India

First edition: 2019

10 9 8 7 6 5 4 3 2 1

Printed in the United States of America.

With love to Arati, Ananya, Amritanshu,
little Akhilesh and Niharika
who always support my academic endeavors

Abstract

Qualitative research contributions have enhanced scope in business management alongside the growth of consumer-centric marketing strategies, which is increasingly getting complex and multidimensional. Qualitative research helps understanding contextual interrelationships in business and cognitive human factors in decision making in business and management. Qualitative research has high value as explorative research tool for moderating intangible information. This book discusses qualitative research modeling and new approaches of qualitative data collection, interpretation of results, reporting, and deriving managerial implications. Qualitative research manages the fundamental challenge in interpreting the complexities associated with consumer behavior, particularly in large diversified marketplace and guides managers. This book presents new insights on conducting qualitative market research. It emphasizes on the application of qualitative research in consumer-centric companies of various categories ranging from multinational companies to niche business organizations. It helps business researchers in drawing contemporary interpretations to the behavioral complexities of consumers. Discussions in the book argue that companies need to consider a broader perspective of marketing research to support marketing decisions derived by understanding consumer behavior using qualitative research methodology.

Keywords

action research; ethnography; evidence-based research; information management; mixed-method research; narrative analytics; qualitative research design; qualitative research

Contents

Preface

Qualitative research practices are growing parallel to quantitative research applications as the market today has been largely influenced by intangible variables, which could be better researched through in-depth inquiries. Consumer behavior is continuously changing, and social media is playing a critical role in determining marketing decisions. Research in the areas of consumer behavior, grapevine effect of social media, and organizational culture can be well studied through qualitative methodology. Qualitative research has emerged today with an enhanced scope in business management in conjunction with the social media driven digital marketing, which is increasingly getting complex and multidimensional. The strength of qualitative research has been evidenced in understanding context and interrelationships of cognitive human factors with decision sciences in business and management. It continues to represent a broad and prevalent set of challenges extended beyond business research to political, economic, and social domains. Qualitative research faces some challenges like quantitative research techniques in terms of validation and generalization of research findings. Qualitative research therefore has increasing potential to determine the human involvement in business and related disciplines. Managers face major challenges in accepting the findings of qualitative research, as they are heterogeneous in analysis and descriptive in nature. The hidden challenge with the qualitative research is to conduct it in a scientific manner and justify claims for its own significance, effectiveness, and derived meaning. It requires a highly active engagement from the researchers, respondents, and managers to conduct qualitative research scientifically and drive a great deal of effort to encapsulate intellectual, practical, physical, and emotional information analytics.

Although contemporary market research practices are scientifically carried out using effective statistical techniques and interpretation of results to support the development of appropriate strategies, qualitative research has high value as explorative research tool for moderating intangible information. Of these, questionnaire structuring, area sampling, and trend analysis are widely adopted techniques in marketing research. An effective information system makes the marketing research a more analytical, fact finding and prolific decision-making exercise. The scope for marketing research is very wide, and it is carried out by identifying potential markets and determining the marketing mix. There are many typologies argued by the marketing research scholars. Marketing research orientation shifts according to different typologies. Motivational research is very significant, and it studies the psychographics or qualitative perspectives of value and lifestyle of consumers. This is a continuum of new skills and ideas that are accredited to marketing research concepts and practices. Marketing research, thus, provides important help to management by supporting decision-making to set objectives, developing an action plan, executing the plan, and controlling its performance.

Despite wider concerns in academics for effective application of qualitative research in the area of marketing, it has been argued that the full potential of qualitative inquiry is not being effectively used. The reason for low preferences to evaluate consumer cognition and managerial perspectives with qualitative inquiry relates to the tendency to promote quantitative methods, though they might not explain clearly the perceptions and values of consumers and employees. These tendencies explain why researchers should choose qualitative methods to address foundational issues. To address the need for qualitative research, this book discusses qualitative research modeling and new approaches of qualitative data collection, interpretation of results, reporting, and deriving managerial implications. Accordingly, this book identifies the strengths and weaknesses of qualitative research methods and argues for the need to reorient business research toward the qualitative inquiry. The discussion model of the book is elaborated in Figure P1.

This book examines the improved qualitative research methods, and emphasizes the application of qualitative research in consumer-centric companies of various categories ranging from multinational companies to niche business organizations. Qualitative research designs discussed in the book refer to decision-making across consumer cultures, analyzing the changing preferences, vogue, and marketplace environment. The book deliberates the role of qualitative research in carrying out customer-

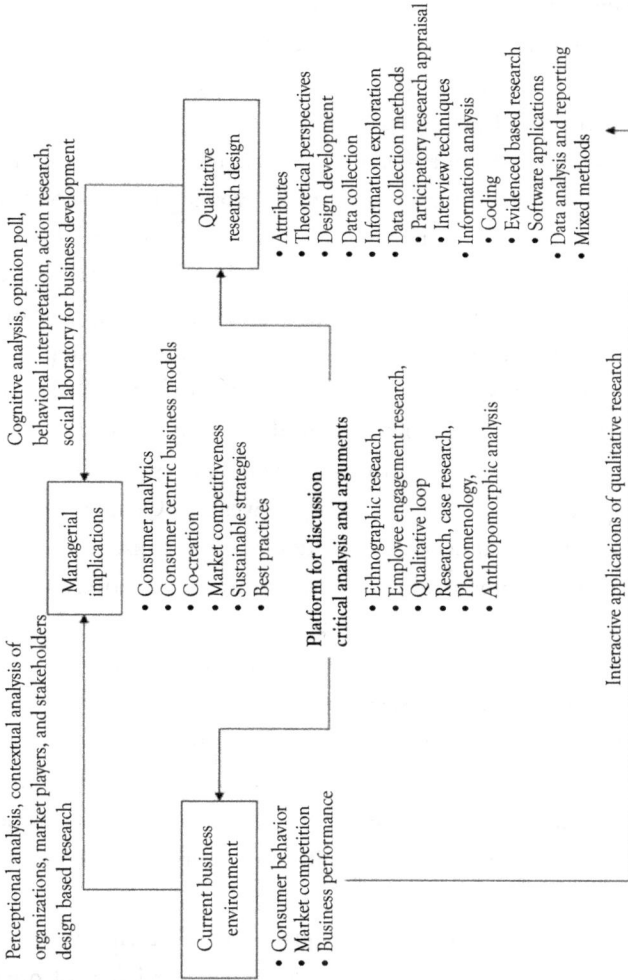

Perceptional analysis, contextual analysis of
organizations, market players, and stakeholders
design based research

Cognitive analysis, opinion poll,
behavioral interpretation, action research,
social laboratory for business development

Managerial implications
- Consumer analytics
- Consumer centric business models
- Cocreation
- Market competitiveness
- Sustainable strategies
- Best practices

Qualitative research design
Attributes
- Theoretical perspectives
- Design development
- Data collection
- Information exploration
- Data collection methods
- Participatory research appraisal
- Interview techniques
- Information analysis
- Coding
- Evidenced based research
- Software applications
- Data analysis and reporting
- Mixed methods

**Platform for discussion
critical analysis and arguments**
- Ethnographic research,
- Employee engagement research,
- Qualitative loop
- Research, case research,
- Phenomenology,
- Anthropomorphic analysis

Current business environment
- Consumer behavior
- Market competition
- Business performance

Interactive applications of qualitative research

Figure P1 Discussion paradigm of the book

oriented strategies, like *Shakti* experiment (2003) of Hindustan Lever Limited in India, which empowered rural women for community marketing of its brands. One of the core arguments presented in this book is to use qualitative methodologies to study brand-associated anthropomorphic analysis, ethnographic research for mapping social needs, desires, and preferences for multinational brands, and phenomenological research to measure the brand reputation in the community.

Marketing strategies can be derived based on qualitative research in reference to the social values, business ambience, and consumer attitudes to understand the consumer cognitive drivers meticulously, and develop synergy with the business strategies. In the growing market competition in the 21st century, corporate success depends on consumer-oriented business strategies formulated by analyzing the consumer psychology. This book presents new insights on conducting and applying qualitative market research. It helps business researchers in drawing contemporary interpretations to the behavioral complexities of consumers. The book also guides corporate managers in developing marketing strategies in reference to time, territory, thrust, target, and tasks (five Ts) focused on the consumers and market competitiveness. Qualitative research helps companies in understanding the emerging consumer behavioral perspectives, developing marketing and operations dexterity, and managing economies of scale, distribution, pricing, and promotion advantages. New enterprise in the global marketplace needs strong management skills for consumer-driven strategies, competitiveness, and assuring sustainable growth. Hence qualitative research needs to be applied in business as a tool for developing consumer-centric strategy. Qualitative research manages the fundamental challenge in interpreting the complexities associated with consumer behavior, particularly in large diversified marketplace and guides managers.

Epistemologically, positivism in qualitative research has diversified to take a cursory or careful look on phenomena or issues of organizational needs, interest, and growth. These phenomena have driven positivism in qualitative research and led through the diversities of knowledge over the past streamlined and rhythmic course of philosophical thinking. In contemporary perspective, globalization has opened many options to manage consumer-oriented business, which prompted companies to understand consumer behavior both intrinsically and extrinsically. Qualitative research has always been found to be the right methodology to understand consumer behavior. Thus, most companies need to understand consumers by associating them in the global marketplace in order to develop collateral work dynamics. The book blends consumer behavior perspectives with qualitative research designs to converge effective business performance and societal values. The book argues that companies need to consider a broader perspective of marketing research to support marketing decisions derived by understanding consumer behavior. This book bridges the methodological perspectives in marketing research with applied marketing decisions putting the consumer first in the business management process.

The concept of qualitative research culture has received widespread attention as a strategic decision tool in marketing management. It is necessary to understand the thematic ambience of research in reference to the rationale of the study, its fitness to the study area, available potential for acquiring information, and anticipated outcome of the research for carrying forward a quality research study. Setting qualitative research scenario is a challenging task for researchers in which research questions, propositions, and constructs of the study need to be developed upon reviewing previous studies. Then, the field research operations of the study could be managed by defining samples for qualitative study, locating the data collection region, developing profile of respondents, and scheduling meetings with the identified samples for acquiring information.

Market research also involves direct observation of customers who are buying and using the products. This method allows companies to know the consumer behavior toward the existing products and develop competitive marketing strategy accordingly. The behavior of consumers toward the existing products gives important clues to customer preferences, especially in mature markets. In markets, where access is free, and the customers have well-developed preferences, the sales records of the various products constitute a shortcut to understanding customer preferences. This method is very useful during the prelaunch stage for the foreign firms to develop an appropriate launch of their products in the segmented markets. The method of observation also faces some practical difficulties if certain assumptions are made to interpret the observed issues. A firm may assume that the current products reflect customer preferences, and such assumption is likely to hold only in mature markets with no entry barriers. However, in markets, where customers have been deprived of products because of trade barriers, consumers might display a preference for something different. Such latent preferences cannot be uncovered through observation. On the other hand, the causal marketing research is sometimes combined with experimental methods of research and causal models. This book serves as a managerial guide to work with the new perspectives of qualitative marketing research.

Understanding the need for qualitative research, business houses today realize that it is essential to support a set of key decisions that collectively determine how companies can develop marketing decisions, perform in the competitive marketplace, and mitigate consumer-led risks. This book argues new dimensions associated with the implications of qualitative research to measure the changing perspectives of consumer preferences, knowledge, values, and organizational decision-making abilities, and addresses several pertinent questions that include the following:

- Why is qualitative research necessary for marketing decision-making?
- How to interpret behavioral and intangible dimensions related to market environment?
- Why should companies make business decisions based on the consumer experience?
- How to make right cognitive analytics for making right decisions in consumer-centric business?
- Why do key decision makers need to read the minds of the stakeholders, and struggle to create value?

This book connects managers to behavioral domain of all the role players in the marketplace and offers a strategic direction in marketing decisions. A faster, cost-effective, and most commonly used method to learn about customers in a market is to do a trade survey by interviewing people in the distribution channels and trade associations. In trade surveys, types of buyers, types of buying processes used, and the sources of buyer information are clearly defined. Professional market research firms can also provide a solution to the multinational companies seeking trade surveys on who the respondents should be, when to administer the questionnaires, what should be the nature of questions, and how many questions should be used in the trade surveys. These market research firms provide a good starting point for further data gathering and analysis. This book also offers qualitative research design for analyzing consumer psychodynamics through peer-to-peer communication, and suggests the decision path. Effective business management begins with selecting and prioritizing the stakeholder needs to support the company's mission and strategy. This book builds knowledge and skills on the theoretical and applied aspects of the qualitative research methods to guide consumer-led business strategies.

This book guides qualitative researchers to learn to see, hear, perceive, and understand in new ways. Students need to learn to move themselves out of the center of their own attention, and clearly observe social settings and the individuals within them. The book guides researchers to learn qualitative research designs to analyze consumer experience. They need to develop a finely tuned ethical sense and negotiate ethical dilemmas encountered in the research process. This book systematically directs researchers to analyze and perceive patterns in the data they collect, so that they can conduct thematic analysis. This book bridges the myths and realities on qualitative research and suggests cognitive analytics-based marketing strategies for building stakeholders value. In the dynamic and competitive marketplace today, a manager's key challenge is coping with frequently changing preferences of consumers and market demand. This book methodologically presents the process of conducting qualitative research with focus on contemporary resources such as digital qualitative analytics, text-data mining, image and verbal data analytics, user-generated content analysis, and opinion breakdown analysis in an organization or a community.

This book provides the knowledge and skills on qualitative research that managers can use to develop consumer-driven marketing strategies. The details on qualitative research theories, study design, information analysis, interpretation of verbal information, and reporting have been explained systematically. Most growing companies have the vision to consistently create or introduce new business initiatives with customers and suppliers, and incorporate consumer opinion database into their enterprise resources planning systems. This book offers knowledge and skills also about developing market-centric and competition-oriented models using qualitative research models. It illustrates the power of qualitative research in managing sensitive market interventions through marketing-mix strategies, innovation, and technology application for expanding and establishing business in competitive markets. The broad foundation of this book is laid on conceptual discussions on qualitative research, and applied arguments toward decision-making in developing marketing strategies. This book categorically reviews qualitative research theories, concepts, and previous researches, and discusses the applied tools and techniques for business decisions. This book significantly contributes to the existing literature and serves as a learning post and a think-tank for students, researchers, and business managers.

Rajagopal

November 09, 2018

Mexico City

Acknowledgments

In completing this volume, I have been benefitted by discussions with my colleagues within and outside EGADE Business School. I am thankful to Dr. Ernesto Amoros, Professor and Associate National Director of Doctoral Program at EGADE Business School, Mexico, who has given me the opportunity to deliver courses on qualitative research in the doctoral program. I thank all my students of graduate and doctoral programs at EGADE Business School for sharing enriching ideas on the subject during classroom discussions, which helped in building this book on the framework of innovative ideas. This book is an outgrowth of my teaching new concepts in qualitative research to doctoral research scholars and working managers in the MBA program.

I also acknowledge the outstanding support of Robin J. Zwettler, Executive Editor of Business Expert Press, who critically examined the proposal, guided the manuscript preparation, and took the publication process forward. My special thanks to Dr. Naresh Malhotra, Regents Professor Emeritus at Scheller College of Business, Georgia Tec University, and series editor on consumer behavior at Business Expert Press, for his guidance and encouragement in bringing out this volume. I am thankful to various anonymous referees of my previous research works on innovation and technology management that helped me in looking deeper into the conceptual gaps and improving the quality with their valuable comments.

Finally, I express my deep gratitude to my beloved wife Arati Rajagopal, who has been instrumental in completing this book like all other works of mine. I acknowledge her help in copyediting the first draft of the manuscript, and for staying in touch till the final proofs were cross-checked and index was developed.

CHAPTER 1

Introduction to Qualitative Research

Overview

Qualitative research is an art of learning from people by analyzing their perceptions, emotions, and neurophysical dynamics concerning social, cultural and personal values, and lifestyle. This is an explorative research tool used through interpersonal discussions and continuous observations of subjects in a given field of study. Qualitative research method has evolved epistemologically across positivism, empiricism, and interpretive schools of thought, which has influenced symbolic interactionism, phenomenology, and ethnographic research streams. Human interactivity, freedom of expressions, emotional manifestation, logic, and rationality in information provide insights into the research problem, and help to interlink ideas through semantic mapping for potential quantitative research. This chapter discusses salient features of qualitative research as a tool and emphasizes the attributes of a good researcher to conduct qualitative research. The core discussions in this chapter are the ecosystem of qualitative research, research planning, and developing research design. In addition, the chapter discusses the evolution of schools of thought in the context of qualitative research.

Introduction

Market research in the growing competitive business environment is a complex phenomenon. There is no single method, which can suffice the dynamic strategy development for companies in the rapidly changing markets. Market research organizations emphasize on data-based quantitative analysis to help companies in making probabilistic decision using various business analytics tools. Various statistical methods are encouraged in the areas of decision sciences to guide marketing research and offer dynamic solutions with the real-time business environment. However, a plethora of data with precise quantitative analytics, sometimes fails to diagnose the complexities in business. Understanding consumer behavior and values are intertwined with the psychosocial, personal, and cognitive complexities. This nucleus focuses the consumer behavior at the hub of the business where every company invests its resources to reach out the consumers over space and time. The underlying challenge in market research is to understand the consumer who is the nucleus of the business ecosystem, and is intertwined with the psychosocial, economic, political, technological, and legal complexities. The consumer yet acts as the pivot of business and overpowers the markets across the regions. Understanding consumer is as complex as knowing the human mind, as the neuroscientists claim that about 10 percent of its total potential has been discovered as on today. Learning from consumers is a grassroots expedition for researchers to explore the emotions, perception, attitude, and behavior that lead to the semantics of decision making within the dynamic of business ecosystem. Interacting with consumers to learn their emotions is central to qualitative inquiries, and mapping the cognitive analytics to guide the market research for an organization is the foundation of qualitative research. Thus, qualitative research is more dynamic, uncertain, and complex, which is beyond the numeric expressions.

Qualitative research draws interpretations of liberal cognitive expressions through a systematic approach to inductive and deductive theories, and thus is essential to the scientific method in the pursuit of knowledge. Qualitative research is an inquiry process based on interpretivism, which focuses on interpretation and meaning of responses collected, and aims to explore social or human problems. The inductive research outgrows through qualitative design of investigation, which believes that the information collected through interviews, storyboard analytics, and observations are prima facie true and can be validated as an expression of the respondent. However, the inductive logic that extends from some observations to all, can never be fully tested or proven due to the lack of homogeneity in the information. Contrary to qualitative research, the deductive process generates conclusions from the generalizations by analyzing the quantitative data. The deductive inquires require interpreting the generalizations though cognitive analytics against the numeric data.

Qualitative research is an ethnographic and phenomenological expedition to measure human values, emotions, and logical narratives. It is an exciting experience and an important way to understand the perceptions of respondents. Mapping the cognitive dynamics of consumers is a highly rewarding activity for researchers as it offers several judgmental moves for making right marketing strategies. The study of cognitive analytics involves neurocentric expressions of market players including manufacturers, suppliers, retailers, consumers, and corporate strategists in the marketing organizations. Qualitative research allows researchers to explore a wide array of dimensions in the sociocultural, behavioral, and business-related domains emerging from the understandings, experiences, and future propositions (Mason 2002). Qualitative inquiries are founded on reasoning and thematic connectivity of arguments entwined in a research domain. Such inquiries are held through in-depth interviews, perceptual mapping, cognitive semantics, and sharing of experiences across spatial and temporal dimensions.

Attributes of Qualitative Research

Qualitative information is a source of well-grounded rich descriptions, which imparts knowledge in identifiable local contexts. Researcher can preserve the chronological flow with qualitative data, map the chronological order of information, events and consequences, and derive fruitful explanations. In general, the attributes of qualitative research methodology are as follows:

- Informal scenario
- Nonprobability-based sampling
- Nongeneralizable sampling
- Circular reasoning
- Formative, earlier phases
- Rich information and time-consuming
- Flexible study design

- Use of adaptive instrument
- Inductive study

Qualitative research is conducted in an informal scenario, which is comfortable to the respondents and researcher. As the qualitative inquiry is based on sharing experiences and forethoughts, and mapping semantics of perceptions, it needs to be organized in a place that respects privacy and personality. Creating an exhibitionistic setup may distract the respondents and restrict the flow of thoughts in a construed ambiance. The most suitable ambiance for qualitative research is the place, which is free from external interventions, dependable, and relaxing. In qualitative research, the focus is mainly on verbal elucidations, facial interpretations, and the researcher's observation. Qualitative research involves an interpretive, naturalistic approach to explore the research themes, which demands qualitative researchers to explore research in the natural settings. Therefore, conducting research in the natural setting of participants would benefit the researchers. It would enable them to interpret phenomena in terms of the meanings embedded in the responses of the subjects. The effects of the environment on conducting qualitative research studies are as discussed as follows:

- Created settings for interviews make respondents conscious and submissive to the researchers. Such ambiences suppress the cognitive emotions and expressions in responding to the questions.
- Researchers can make relevant assumptions by understanding the quality of life and psychosocial determinants of respondents in a natural environment.
- Openness of mind is largely influenced by ergonomic settings for interviews against expressing in a natural way. For instance, a studio setting of a television interview affects the psychoneurotic conditions of a casual interviewee.
- Conversations with respondents adapting to their existing quality of life conditions influence behavioral attributes. Therefore, ethnographic way of research is considered to be an effective tool for conducting qualitative research, where a

researcher plans to live with the respondents adapting to their socio-economic and cultural settings, and

- Researchers can build acquaintance with the subjects in a real-life conditions.

Selection of respondents for qualitative research is widely based on the attributes of respondents, their convenience, and the purpose of the study. Sampling for qualitative research is not based on the probability proportion of the population. Data collection and analysis in qualitative research consists of conducting in-depth interviews, documenting direct observation, and analyzing verbal and nonverbal information like written documents, images, and storyboards. Researchers prefer purposive or snowballing (referred) sampling as qualitative research is built around nonprobabilistic samples. However, in a comprehensive quantitative research, the goal would be to conduct a random sampling that ensures that the sample group would be representative of the entire population, and therefore, the results could be generalized to the entire population. Such qualitative research involves high cost and long time to complete the qualitative research projects. Thus, the goal of qualitative research is generally set to provide in-depth understanding targeting a specific group, type of individuals, event or process. To accomplish this goal, qualitative research focuses on criterion-based sampling techniques to reach their target group (Berg and Lune 2004). Commonly, most qualitative researches are conducted with limited samples based on the convenience of the researcher, or in accordance with the research situation. The qualitative analytics of such studies cannot be generalized.

Qualitative responses are sometimes ambiguous, which leads to circular reasoning for drawing interpretations during the study. Ambiguity in responses is caused due to rhetoric questions, social and personal sensitivity, and revealing the classified politico-legal information. Circular reasoning leads to logical fallacy in which the researcher makes a presumption about the right response. In circular reasoning, analysis of facts begins with the speculation about the answer with which a respondent is trying to conclude the conversation. The components of circular arguments are often argumentative, speculative, and need to be logically validated by testing whether the conceived premises are true. However, in qualitative investigation, good informal arguments offer justification for most conclusions. Respondents go wrong if the arguments are reversed in a related statement or response of the same person tends to be unfit in a similar situation. Such responses make the arguments circular. Circularity, however, is not necessarily the only property of an argument in qualitative research, it may depend on how often the argument repeats an earlier claim, and whether the repetition occurs justifying the same argument or response across the qualitative inquiry. Therefore, before ruling an argument as circular, it is necessary to establish whether the claim is properly grounded in agreed-upon information (Rips 2002).

Qualitative research is a flexible process, which allows researcher to modify existing research propositions and formulate new propositions that are more appropriate during the study process. Therefore, the qualitative research remains flexible and formative during the early phases. Though qualitative inquiries are time-consuming, they provide rich information for analysis. Researchers use adaptive instrument for study ecosystem and develop the inductive researcher process laid on grounded theory. Qualitative research is a real-time investigation, which is based on quality of information and observations of researchers for interpreting the responses under various scenarios. A qualitative researcher should adhere to clarity in analytics by validating the responses and maintaining an unbiased state of mind throughout the process of research.

Qualitative information analyzed through user groups, interviews, and field observation serves as a powerful tool to understand consumer desires and motivations. IKEA, a Swedish popular retailer of home furnishings has the philosophy of co-creating designs understanding the consumer needs, emotions, and values. The company relies widely on the qualitative inquiries through focus groups and informal interviews about the existing and latent needs, and preferences of consumers. IKEA extensively uses the qualitative customer research to create products that are of high perceived use value and offer comparative social status. IKEA does not just add value to its products, it reinvents it through learning from customer by conducting focus group discussions periodically. The systematic qualitative inquiries with the key players in the market help the company to reconfigure roles and relationships among suppliers, partners, and customers and mobilize creation of value by new combinations of different perceptions, emotions, and values in co-creating business.

Several ideas, responses, and observations emerge during the in-depth interviews with respondents, so a skilled researcher should engage in carrying out perceptual mapping and semantics during the study. Perceptual mapping would help the researcher map the flow of responses against the principal and interrelated questions. Joining several responses to the related questions on perceptual map can guide the researcher in determining the state of emotions (like happiness, sadness, anger, commanding, aggressive, defensive, and submissiveness). Interpreting emotions in qualitative research leads to establish the thrust of responses—vertical (self-image congruity) and horizontal (social-image congruity). The thrust in responses reinforces the respondents' involvement in the research and the commitment in responses. The contours of perceptual map indicate high involvement, correctness, and self-validation of responses during the qualitative interviews.

Attributes of a Researcher

A good researcher develops semantic map on the interconnecting words outgrowing from the responses during the in-depth interviews in the qualitative research process. Semantics is concerned with interconnected words, and their meaning and contextual relevance in the research. The formal semantics is the study of logical aspects of meaning such as sense, reference, and implication within the context of the research study. The logical and lexical semantics studies the word meanings and their etymological relations within the research domain, while the conceptual semantics studies the cognitive structure of meaning. The qualitative researchers can follow any of the suitable semantics methods to develop a semantic map during the interviews, and interpret the semantics during the information analysis of qualitative inquiry. Prior to beginning the qualitative inquiry, researchers need to be well acquainted with the study area by understanding the basic dispositions of people around, and their ethnic, social, and cultural values. Making judgments based on the self-reference or invalidated referrals may cause biasness among researchers toward respondents and their responses. Nonetheless, the attributes of good researchers should include the following traits:

- Experience
- Rationale
- Empathy
- Judgmental behavior
- Minimizing biases
- Peer influence
- Interception and mediation
- Developing thematic conversation pathway, streamlining, interpreting emotions
- Exploring concealed sense in conversation

It is necessary for researchers to possess considerable experience on the subject matter, study area, cognitive analytics, and documenting appropriate observations to carry out the qualitative research studies. They should also exhibit rationale in analyzing information and empathy to respondents during the interview. However, researchers conducting qualitative inquiry need to be indifferent toward making any judgments, as such behavior induces biasness. The peer influence also needs to be avoided, as it make the researchers judgmental and biased toward the respondents in particular and the social group in general. Qualitative researchers do not start with a theory that they aim to test. Instead, they explore rationale in the responses and work on inductive concepts to support the grounded theory of the study. They often work the other way around seeking more evidential information to support the theory with data despite methodological limitations.

One of the principal attributes of a qualitative researcher is to learn to see, hear, perceive and visualize the respondent's forethoughts, and understand from the perspectives of the interviewee. The researcher needs to learn to stay at par with the respondents, move himself out of the center of his own attention, and clearly adapt to social settings and the peers. Interpreting meanings from the perspectives of others is an art, and the qualitative researcher should develop such skill. He needs to develop a finely tuned ethical sense and negotiate ethical dilemmas encountered in the research process, and be able to analyze and perceive patterns of the information inflow to conduct thematic analysis. Successful qualitative researcher remains open to the eventualities during the interview process, is honest in action and reflection, and develops a sense of multiple realities. Empowering the subjects or respondents pays a big dividend to the researcher as he gains more time to listen and observes the proceedings. A researcher, who asks questions, should allow other to talk and intercept the subject at some point. Following the lead in discussion and observing the grapevine effect, new topics are introduced among the peers that may provide innovative opening to the research. The skilled researcher will let the other person lead the conversation despite the personal limitations (Hill 2007).

Qualitative research can be conducted successfully, if the researcher has experience on the subject, acquaintance in the study area, and ability to analyze the responses rationally. Rationale is a subjective domain in the qualitative research, which leads to cognitive sophistication among the researchers. Some studies establish that the rationale and cognitive sophistication have strong connotation. Cognitive sophistication can be explained as the cognitive ability reflected in the functional intelligence connecting various thinking dispositions such as open-mindedness and superstitious thinking (Toplak, West, and Stanovich 2014). Rationality is the fundamental analytical sphere to the understanding of mind and behavior, which is the core of qualitative research. Therefore, some of the basic attributes of a qualitative researcher is to have intuitive sense and inductive reasoning to understand human behavior. A researcher should also exhibit reflective equilibrium to drive a wedge between formality and normativity during the conversations and documenting the responses (Chater and Oaksford 2000). A researcher conducting qualitative studies and engaged in the in-depth interviews should have the ability to understand and share the feelings of respondents. It is necessary for a researcher to be empathetic toward respondents during the study, as such behavior would inculcate the sense of familiarity among respondents and build confidence. During the process of qualitative study, a researcher should never be judgmental under the influence of personal and social bias, or peer effect.

Interception and mediation in qualitative inquiries are considered as good attributes, but they need to be performed on need basis. Interceptions in survey have two dimensions. First, choosing respondents randomly from the crowd, which is a casual way to collect information by abrupt interviewing; and second, intercepting the response of an interviewee by asking questions outgrowing over the responses during the interview process. In qualitative research, conversation pathways should be prepared prior to setting the interviews with respondents by prioritizing the interview questions and their respective logical connectivity. During the interview, a researcher can create a storyboard to map the conversation, which would help in developing sequential interpretations of responses. However, in descriptive interviews, respondents often enjoy the liberty of expressions, which may take the responses astray and make it difficult to extract the sensible points out of the conversation. Hence, it is necessary for the researcher to streamline the conversation and control the emotions of respondents spanning beyond the interview protocol. Often respondents share unclear information on sensitive questions to the researcher, which are generally categorized as ambiguous responses. A skilled researcher can be able to extract the underlying sense out of such responses by recording the conversation and listening to it carefully.

Qualitative research is usually enjoyed as liberal speaking and listening exercise. However, it could be successful if planned in a scientific way. The researcher should focus on the data collection process, which is central to the subject. Among various qualitative tools, a researcher can use conversations, audiovisual sources, and observations. Filtering of information is necessary in qualitative research as researchers deviate from, and lose, the primary focus due to a lot of supplementary information. In qualitative inquiries, researchers receive plethora of information, arguments and counterarguments, and innovative ideas. However, researchers can make contemporary interpretations provided they critically analyze the arguments and categorically document the respondents' focus and researchers' criticism. Information acquired through interviews should be filtered for multiplicity of meaning and crossover arguments. There should be systematic retrieval of information during the analysis process within the developed information layouts. In qualitative research studies, information from all documented and digitally recorded sources should be retrieved considering the timeliness, comprehensiveness, transparency, repeatability, and confidentiality. Researchers should ensure that the information and related evidence gathered are up-to-date and comprehensive. The information gathered should be in a transparent environment, confidential and anonymous. No information of qualitative interviews should be made public unless authorized in particular. Repeatability of information also needs to be checked while retrieving the qualitative information (Russell-Rose, Chamberlain, and Azzopardi 2018). Transcribing the research notes, recorded information, descriptive contents, and storyboards is one of the complex tasks in the qualitative research method. Information collected during qualitative interviews needs to be arranged in a draft table for each question of the research instrument, which allows to selectively pick the information for analysis. The pattern of information transcription layout is exhibited in Table 1.1, which enables the researcher to identify the core, peripheral, and overlapping information for using them appropriately to generate final research output.

The table illustrates the analytics of each question asked to the respondents in a qualitative research process. Accordingly, the text of core arguments, peripheral description, intercept responses, and overlapping responses need to be documented. The decision matrix for each question needs to be assessed to determine its strength and weakness. This should be done in reference to the researcher's ranking on emotions associated with the response, extent of biasness, and originality of responses to check whether it is original or adopted. The peripheral description to a question such as "who do you like to be a leader for the country?" can be the response that describes about the political parties in the country and their attributes. The intercept response to the core arguments in the earlier context may be in reference to the intercept question-"why did you say so." The reasons given by the respondent need to be documented in the column "intercept responses" to delineate the cause and effect of the core argument(s). Respondents often validate their arguments by citing their experience, expressing self-image congruity, giving anthropomorphic explanations, or by presenting social validation. The validated responses should be documented in the table. Such analysis for each question in the qualitative research process would help the researcher in admitting

Table 1.1 Sample information transcription layout-question#

Observations	Core arguments	Peripheral descriptions	Intercept responses	Overlapping arguments	Validated response	Researcher's Ranking		
						Emotions (H-M-L-N)	Biasness (H-M-L-N)	Originality (Y-A-N)
1								
2								
3								
4								
5								

H, High; M, Moderate; L, Low; Y, Yes; A, Adopted; N, Not Defined.

the observations for the psychometric, cognitive, or opinion analytics of the study.

Qualitative Research Ecosystem

Social sciences have widely encouraged qualitative research methods to enable researchers to study social and cultural phenomena embedded in the society. However, this method has been extended to psychology and human studies over time. Almost every research field and area has adopted the use of qualitative method and analysis today. As discussed earlier, qualitative research method involves data collection of personal experiences, introspection and narrations about life, interviews, observations, interactions, and visual texts that are significant in socioeconomic, political, cultural, and human studies. A specified ecosystem supported by the grounded theory, governs such research studies. Grounded theory is an inductive methodology developed through a systematic generation of assumptions from a set of interpersonal research tools and observations, which is determined as the conceptual background, and serves as the foreground for data collection and analysis. The ecosystem of qualitative research therefore embeds the grounded theory, and sociocultural and political environment at the background; while the research setting, development of research instrument, quality of information, arguments and validations, audiovisual aides, and the observation of researcher form the foreground of research. Figure 1.1 exhibits the elements of qualitative research ecosystem.

Qualitative research needs immense interpersonal skills for acquiring information on the topic of research, drawing observations, and developing an appropriate grounded theory, which can be validated through predetermined propositions as exhibited in Figure 1.1. Grounded theory involves the identification and integration of research propositions from the analysis of preliminary data (pilot test), or review of previous studies. It is both the process of developing propositions and integration (as method), and its output (as theory). Thus, it can be stated that the grounded theory is an inductive research method constructed based on the principal phenomenon and tested through the data that has been systematically collected and analyzed. It is used to uncover the social,

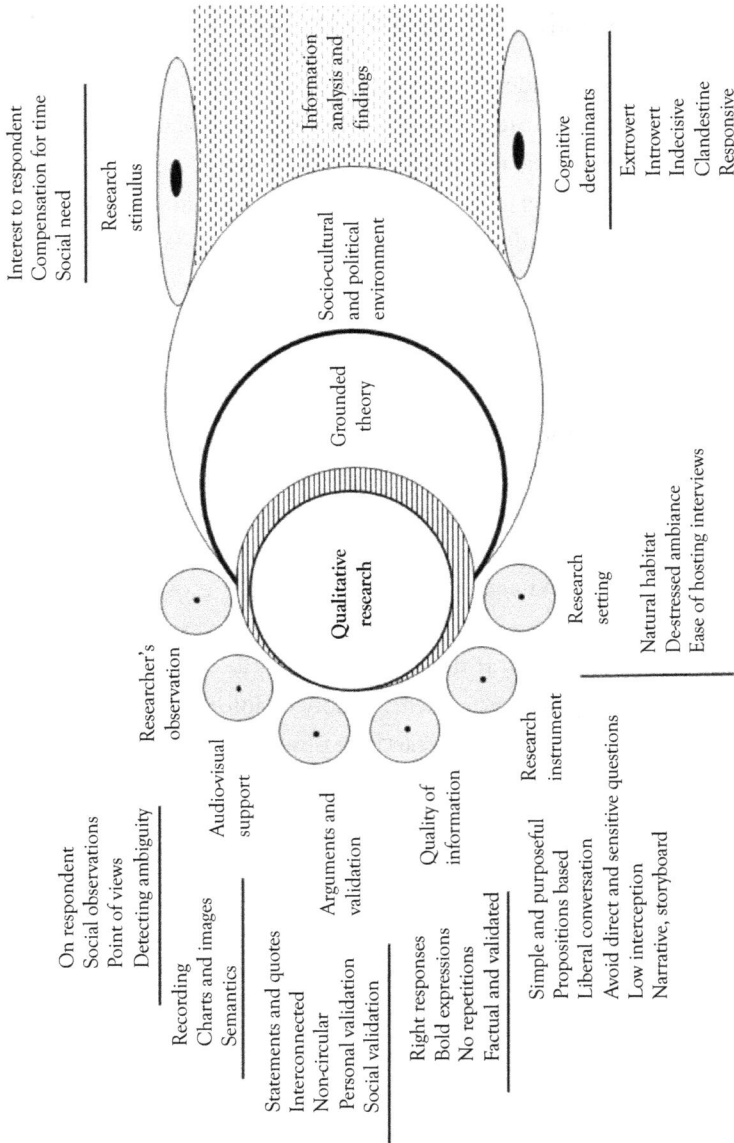

Figure 1.1 Qualitative research ecosystem

interpersonal, and peer relationships that emerge in a social process. The following are the features of grounded theory (Charmaz 1995):

- Data collection and analysis are carried out simultaneously within a predetermined period of study.
- Categories and analytic codes are developed from data within theoretical sensitivity (researcher's insights) by using conceptual models derived from observations or review of previous studies.
- Theoretical sampling is used to refine categories.
- Research propositions, data collection, and analytical tools are constructed inductively.
- Social processes are discovered in the data.
- Analytical memos are used between coding and writing.
- The principal phenomenon is integrated in developing the theoretical framework.

In order to test the grounded theory through qualitative research methodology, the data collection process needs to be set in a natural habitat, where the subjects (respondents) stay at ease, and could participate in the interview without any stress, as illustrated in Figure 1.1. The data can be collected through a simple and purposeful research instrument. It is important to understand that a large number of questions may disrupt the information as it may affect the respondents by creating confusion. Once the grounded theory is developed and propositions are finalized, the questions in the research instrument should be consistent with both the grounded theory and its propositions. The questions should be framed in the way that they prompt for liberal conversation, and encourage narrative or story like information. In doing so, the direct and sensitive questions need to be avoided. However, a researcher's interception during the interview process is a healthy trend, but it should be done in a moderate way without disrupting the interviewees.

A good research instrument is capable of delivering quality information. The attributes of quality information include right and validated responses, and bold expressions. Generally, if the questions asked during the interview are similar, there are possibilities of repetitions in the responses, which need to be filtered before subjecting it to data analysis. In qualitative research, the most complex exercise is arraying the arguments embedded in the information. As discussed in Table 1.1, the arguments should be extracted from the information, and interrelationship among various statements (described as arguments) should be established. Circularity in reasoning of the statements should be eliminated, or if it is difficult to do so, such statements should be excluded from the analysis. Researchers should try to get all statements validated through social or self-image congruity. Use of audiovisual aides during data collection process would help researchers in recording the data, and later transcribe it to develop charts and semantics of ideas and arguments as illustrated in Figure 1.1. The observations of researchers on the personality of respondents, their personal point of views, and societal views also play significant role in information analysis. However, it is important to detect and remove ambiguities before putting the data through the analytical process.

Consumer-centric companies today are reorienting their strategy development process from top-down to bottom-up paradigms through continuous learning from the stakeholders and role players in their business about their perceptions, attitude, and behavior. They follow qualitative research tools to document ongoing face-to-face interactions and to analyze the user-generated content on the digital platforms. These practices have helped companies including PNC bank (USA), IKEA (Sweden), and Ambuja Cements (India) bring discipline and coherence to their customer relations management and product portfolios. Burberry, the fashion design company in the United Kingdom, which is widely regarded for its apparel and fashion accessories portfolios, ensures the voice of the customer (VOC). The VOC projects are conducted periodically through opinion surveys and within the qualitative research ecosystem.

Qualitative Research Plan

Previous studies claim that qualitative research is an outgrowth of Plato's "arch of knowledge." The arch of knowledge demonstrates that any scientific method of knowledge building is essentially based on induction and deduction processes. Qualitative research systematically generates knowledge by planning appropriate study design. Thus, qualitative research solidifies the arch of knowledge, which is based on two pillars: (i) interviews, observations, and textual data, and (ii) interpretation and meaning founded on predictions and explanations. These two pillars are linked with theories, concepts, and models than can be created (inductive research) or tested (deductive research) through data analysis, interpretation, and explanations (Chalmers 1982). Over time, therefore, "qualitative research" has become a familiar and useful research technique, which privileges those social and business processes that cannot be easily quantified or codified using numerical classifications such as interpretation processes, sense-making, meaning-making, situated actions, discursive constructions, processes, contextual factors, interactions, or interpersonal dynamics (Fletcher, Massis, and Nordqvist 2016).

Planning for successful qualitative research depends on the contemporary relevance of the research topic in social, economic, and business domains, which could generate enough interpersonal dynamics for acquiring information. The relevance of research topic needs to be supported by the quality of information, timeliness, and completeness of the data analytics. Qualitative research can be planned in the following sequential stages as exhibited in Table 1.2.

Often qualitative research generates propositions to be tested with the descriptive information analysis. The research problems determining the core and peripheral issues extend from cognitive to business related topic in qualitative methodology as discussed in Table 1.2. Therefore, qualitative studies are invaluable in new fields of study, and are often used in developing theories or conceptual frameworks. The researcher should develop an appropriate statement of the research problem emphasizing the core and peripheral issues that need to be addressed during the research. A clear statement of research problems will guide the researcher in developing right instrument for an appropriate research design. There are four types of research designs comprising experimental, dynamic, explorative, and casual research designs.

Table 1.2 Stages of qualitative research planning

Sequence	Stage	Description
1	Identifying problem	Cognitive, sociocultural, business related, socio-economic, innovation and technology, political, relationships, business governance, and so on.
2	Developing appropriate statement of problem	Core and peripheral issues
3	Justification of research	Validation of problem statement
4	Research design	Experimental, dynamic, explorative, or casual
4.1	Sampling	Random, snowballing, stratified, cluster, probability proportional to size
4.2	Data Collection	In-depth interviews, observation, text mining, opinion analytics, official documents
5	Data processing and analysis	Data transcription, data validation, filtering information, content analysis, semantics, and critical factor analysis
6	Developing research report	Presentation of results, developing storyboards, interpretation of statements and arguments, managerial/ policy implications, action points, conclusion and limitations of the study, and future research perspectives

Research Designs

The experimental designs are characterized by the random selection of participants to administer a predetermined or random assignment of the participants in a groups study. The participatory research appraisal (PRA) is an experimental design wherein the participants are engaged in an exercise of common interest. Qualitative research projects on socioeconomic development employ the PRA to the rural, semiurban, or urban habitants to find out the community perspectives. The researcher also conducts controlled group experiments by moderating the extraneous variables. Dynamic research designs are developed with variations in the dependent and independent variables woven around the broad research theme. The dynamic research designs are developed using brainstorming sessions and causal loop diagrams derived out of these sessions. Such research design is used for the subjects (respondents) who have multiple dimensions to express the final output. One of the right examples to explain the dynamic research design is conducting qualitative research in the health sector with an objective to know the satisfaction of patients on a chronic ailment. In this case, the casual loop diagrams drawn during the preliminary round of conversations with the subject may determine what is important for them to get the treatment—cost of treatment (low), abilities of doctor (high), auxiliary support like nursing (affordable), insurance support (high), or life-expectancy (prolonged). Different respondents may have different focuses on carrying out conversation. Accordingly, the dependent variable will change in reference to the subjects. Such qualitative researches are largely consolidated as case studies in a thematic research volume.

Explorative research designs are commonly used in qualitative research, in which comprehensive information is obtained and analyzed. Such research designs are developed to fit into the overall scenario of the research including spatial and temporal aspects. Causal research, which is also called explanatory research, refers to the investigation of cause-and-effect relationships. In order to determine causality, researchers observe variation in the independent variables to measure its impact on another variable(s). It is very complex to conduct casual research using qualitative tools, as it needs robust statistical support. However, qualitative input is also entertained in the casual research design where mixed methodologies (quantitative and qualitative) are used.

Sampling Techniques

Qualitative research usually encourages random sampling within specified criteria for the subjects like age, gender, education, income, and occupation. Any subject may be chosen for interview casually or with prior appointment in random sampling. The interviews are administered in the sampling design for short time using a purposeful research instrument. Snowballing technique is used to select potential subjects for conducting in-depth interviews. Snowball sampling is a referral sampling where subjects of an existing study recruit or suggest potential subjects within their acquaintances. The referred subjects cooperate with the researcher as they hold a trustworthy reference. Stratified sampling is a predetermined number based on the classification of attributes of total population. The classification of subjects is based on social, economic, cultural, and personality-led attributes. The subjects are chosen for the study according to a predetermined proportion out of the total population. In other words, stratified sampling is a method in which the total population is divided into smaller groups or strata. Each stratum is based on some common attributes of the population. After dividing the population into categories, samples should be selected randomly within the categories. Cluster sampling is usually done by pooling the respondents across geo-demographic segments. Sample size of population can be determined at current time by taking appropriate proportion of the predetermined data. For example, using extrapolation method to the population census data, the sample population of the study area can be appropriated for the current time to know the total size. The required proportion of the sample population can be selected from the extrapolated population size at the current time. This method is known as probability proportional to size (PPS). Probability sampling requires that each member of the survey population has a chance of being included in the sample, but it does not require that this chance be the same for everyone. In using this sampling technique, it is not necessary to have an accurate count of population.

Data Collection

In-depth interviewing is a principal qualitative research technique that involves conducting intensive conversations with a small number of respondents to explore their perspectives on a given theme or topic of research. In-depth interviews are useful when there is a need to comprehensively document thoughts and behaviors to explore perceptions and semantics of the subjects. Interviews are often used in context to any experience, or to offer a vision on potential development or technology concerns. In-depth interviews are usually conducted face-to-face and involve one interviewer and one participant. Ideally, interviews should be conducted in a location mutually convenient for the researcher and interviewee with no outsiders present, and where people feel that their confidentiality is completely protected.

Participant observation is commonly used in both anthropological and sociological studies. In qualitative research, observation supplements the information obtained through interviews. Observations enable the researcher to describe the existing situations using the five senses to enhance the value of information and its interpretation. Anthropologists and ethnographic researchers use participant observation as the primary method during their fieldwork, which involves active looking, improving memory, informal interviewing, writing detailed field notes with rationale, and sincerity and patience. Therefore, observation is regarded as a continuous learning tool on the behavior of participants and their surroundings (Kawulich 2005).

Another upcoming method used for acquiring information in qualitative research is text mining or text data mining, which refers to text analytics process that derives high-quality information from online or in-print text. It is a process of analyzing voluminous and unstructured text data through the software, which can identify concepts, patterns, topics, keywords, and other attributes in the data. The text analytics is an application-enabled process of using text-data mining techniques for sorting out contents through data sets. However, empirical research papers on topics related to social sciences and humanities are highly difficult to summarize due to the large volume of literature, and the information scattered over similar topics and databases such as catalogs of collections and sequential databases. In addition, the lack of structure and standards in the sources also makes the text mining a difficult proposition. The textual information is expressed in unstructured, natural language form at different levels of precision, which is difficult for researchers to analyze. Knowledge resources such as controlled vocabularies, taxonomies, and ontologies bring a partial solution to the online keyword-based searches. Knowledge-based search engines extend simple string matching with queries on general terms that do not depend on how they are expressed in the text. However, new text mining and knowledge representation technologies that tackle these problems are emerging (Chaix et al. 2018). Opinion analytics is an outgrowth of opinion mining exercise like text mining. Opinions of business leaders, political leaders, and newspaper editors are harvested by the qualitative researchers online through text data mining software such as Rapid Miner and QDA Miner.

Research Design

Setting qualitative research scenario is a challenging task for researchers, in which research questions, propositions, and constructs of the study need to be developed upon reviewing the previous studies. The field research operations of the study can be managed by defining samples for the qualitative study, locating the data collection region, developing profiles of respondents, and scheduling meetings with the identified samples to acquire information. Some researchers begin data collection process by organizing focus groups to identify variables of the study for developing research instrument. Data collections process then begins by conducting survey or interviews, using the research instrument. Information acquired for the study then needs to be validated to ensure that there is no redundancy and biasness in the data. However, developing scale and the instrument, and data collection should be done in contextual reference to the predetermined objectives of research. Some critical aspects in data collection and management of information include resource use based on cost and time, quality of information, and use of appropriate filters to prepare the data for analysis. The information analysis in qualitative research demands a robust content analysis. Some researchers also use descriptive statistics, if possible, while quantifying the small qualitative samples. Graphic and pictorial illustrations are also extensively used in analysis and reporting of findings of the qualitative information. However, it is very essential for researchers to check the consistency of findings with the predetermined propositions of the study.

Any qualitative research design has the following components, each of which addresses a different set of issues essential to the coherence of a study, as discussed as follows:

- *Goals:* A researcher should set up the goals of the study considering its implications in the industry or society. The goals of the study should be stated in the contexts of why this study is worth doing, what problems are aimed at, and how this study contributes to the existing literature. Researcher may also like to clarify how this qualitative research would influence what practices and policies among the business activities.

- *Conceptual framework*: It is necessary for a researcher to develop conceptual framework based on the issues, settings, or respondents involved in study. Such framework should discuss the relevant theories, beliefs, and prior research findings to develop an appropriate research model. The review of literature, case studies, and personal experiences would also contribute in developing the conceptual framework of the study.

- *Research questions*: A research instrument containing questions to acquire required information from the respondents is the most critical tool in qualitative research. The relevance of questions would help the respondents in expressing their opinion justifiably, and would appeal the researcher to use the acquired data for analysis. The research questions should aim at the information required to analyze and achieve the objectives of the study.

- *Methods*: Research design should determine the right method for conducting the study. It should specify the approaches and techniques for collecting and analyzing the data, and measuring the consistency of results with the research propositions set for the study.

- *Validity*: In qualitative research, the information is largely raw, unfiltered, and to some extent, nonevidenced. Hence, it is challenging to validate the information by applying several crosschecks. It is necessary to determine the plausible alternative interpretations and validity threats to data, and ways to deal with the available data.

Qualitative research must be conducted systematically and rigorously, and should be accountable for its quality and its claims. A flexible research design, which is contextual to the predetermined objectives, contributes to the success of qualitative research. Essentially, this means that the qualitative researchers should not only make decisions by developing a sound research design, but also stay sensitive to the ecosystem of qualitative research comprising the study area, respondents, questionnaire, code of ethics, and to the changing contexts in which the research takes place.

Qualitative research should involve critical self-scrutiny of information, or exhibit active reflexivity during the data collection process. Accordingly, researchers should constantly take stock of their actions, informants' attitude, and their role in the research process, and refine the information acquisition modalities accordingly. However, at times, a researcher cannot be neutral, or objective, or detached, from the knowledge and evidences that are being generated during the data collection process. Researchers conducting qualitative studies should seek to understand their role in the process, stay proactive, interactive, or reactive, and exhibit reflexivity to moderate the qualitative responses (Rajagopal 2018).

Qualitative research should be able to produce arguments, explanations, and new concepts on the research questions rather than claiming to offer numerical evidences with lame descriptions. However, it is more difficult to reach stronger analytical evidences in qualitative research to generalize the findings, as compared to the quantitative approaches. Researchers engaged in qualitative studies should be satisfied with the emerging explanations, which are idiosyncratic or accurate only to the limited empirical parameters of their study. Such attribute of the qualitative research does not underplay the capacity of qualitative methods to facilitate cross-contextual generalities mentioned earlier. Accordingly, undertaking qualitative research studies should not be viewed as a unified body of philosophy and practice, wherein the research methods can be combined unbiasedly. Similarly, qualitative research should not necessarily be regarded opposite to quantitative research (Rajagopal 2018).

Schools of Thought in Qualitative Research

Qualitative research leads to continuous learning through perceptual mapping and semantic analysis of opinions, causes and results, and psychosocial emotions. The information in qualitative research emerges from the various situations, and learning is stimulated at two ends: learning from positive opinions and learning from negative emotions. In order to guide qualitative research, both the learning ends are meaningful, as learning from success leads to develop a positive model, while learning from failures build corrective models in qualitative research. Interpretation of qualitative information is influenced by logical positivism, which grows on the cause-and-effect interrelationship. Positivism in epistemo-logical growth in qualitative research is embedded as theory over time. Positivism and sociology have a common origin, and positivism remains a significant approach for qualitative research in sociology and other social sciences. In positivist sociology, the scientific study of society is identified with empirical research and often social life is inquired through the in-depth conversation to document variety of experiences of subjects (Outhwaite 2015).

Positivism in management research can be witnessed in the synthesis and logical expressions in investigation, unveiled by the judgmental values. Positivism today is beyond the philosophical notions that support the management research based on the assumptions and critical learning. The leaning of management researchers toward positivism cannot be overlooked today, just because they are trekking off the philosophical knowledge and theoretical boundaries. In fact, positivism in the management research has diversified to take a cursory or careful look on phenomena or issues of organizational needs, interest, and growth. These phenomena have driven positivism in management research, and led through the diversities of knowledge over the past streamlined and rhythmic course of philosophical thinking (Ogbo and Kifordu 2015). The contemporary positivism is laid on the foundations of logical positivism and logical empiricism developed in the early 20th century. Its goal is to develop management as a unified science using methodical and logical analysis to unmask traditional philosophical problems of generalizing empirical analysis.

The taxonomy of theories can be found spread across the subjects related to behavior, organization, business, and entrepreneurship that establish convergence with the classical, neoclassical, and modern management thinkers. The positivists, who had built their arguments steering the realistic social, economic, and political situations, advocate bottom-up management philosophy that upholds the voice of stakeholders in a society or in an organization. Positivism in management research in the post-20th century entails attention on the existing social and organizational perspectives instead of analyzing the theses and antitheses of historical epistemology. Mindfulness is the essence of positivism, which enables people to recognize and take advantage of opportunities when they arise, and to avert risk (Rajagopal 2017; Langer and Beard 2014). Over the years, empiricism has been associated with the qualitative research, which has emerged from the experimental sciences in management. The theory of empiricism explains that all knowledge is derived from cognitive science and converges management and action. Researchers experience empiricism in qualitative research in which enlightenment of thought process drives complex and contemplating minds to the new challenges, and induces radicalism in the epistemological development in management research over the conventional thoughts of schools (Rajagopal 2017).

Theoretical concepts that support qualitative research have evolved over a range of factors connecting ontology and epistemology. Ontology is a set of concepts and categories in a subject area or domain such as sociology, that shows attributes like beliefs and ethnology, and their codependency. The qualitative research has grown over the social ontological concepts and the ways to study them with the support of the logical and philosophical phenomena (epistemology). The purpose and goal of the research, the characteristics of research participants, the audience for the research, the sponsors, and the positions and environments of the researchers themselves have become the elements of qualitative research evolving out of classical, neoclassical, and modern schools of thought (Ritchie et al. 2013). Differences in the mix of these factors have led to numerous variations in approaches to qualitative research. Therefore, it is argued that a better quality work is produced if flexible approaches and methods are considered, and choices are made according to the objectives and context of the qualitative research (Seale et al. 2007).

Most epistemological philosophies have common attributes as exhibited in Table 1.3, which would reveal the path of epistemological evolution from traditional to modernist and later toward critical theory.

Critical theory has made a docile stance in management research, while its philosophy has been well established in social research and literature studies. Formalism, which stemmed out of the critical theory, examines the relationships between a texted idea and its form between what a text says and the way it says it. However, critical theory aims at diagnosing the problems of the modern society and prescribing necessary social changes toward reducing the socioeconomic inequality. Philosophically,

Table 1.3 Attributes of embedded philosophies influenced qualitative research over the past

Epistemological evolution	Philosophical and theoretical schools of thought		
	Conventionalism	**Postmodernism**	**Critical theory**
Attributes	• Social paradigms • Knowledge as phenomenon • Constructing research theories • Religion and truth	• Evidence-based research • Linguistic concerns • Relativism • Deconstruction of subject • Goal-oriented research	• Political, socio-cultural, and value oriented • Predictions and control • Emancipation
Synthesis	• Consensus on truth • Observability	• Linguistic importance • Subjectivity	• Empirical knowledge • Social research

critical theory supports communism as evidenced in the Marxism and classical socialist principles (Rajagopal 2017; Layder 1994).

A qualitative research is often described as a naturalistic, interpretive approach, concerned with exploring the perceptions of research participants as a starting point (Flick 2009). The term "qualitative," addresses the concerns with "what," "why," and "how" questions, and focuses on processes and perspectives in qualitative research design. Qualitative approaches are developed around three main constructs of the schools of thought:

- Symbolic interactionism
- Phenomenology
- Ethnography

Symbolic Interactionism

Symbolic interactionism is the view of social behavior that emphasizes linguistic or gestural communication and its subjective understanding, especially the role of language in the formation of a child as a social being. Symbolic interactionists are more concerned with subjective interpretations of perceptions, opinion, and meaningful interactions among individuals. Symbolic interaction occurs within a particular social and cultural context, which are defined and categorized based on individual narratives, emotions, and perceptual meanings. Symbolic interaction examines the meanings emerging from the reciprocal interaction of individuals within social environment and during in-depth conversations with other individuals. The analysis of conversation focuses to find out which symbols and meanings emerge from the interaction between respondents during the research process (Aksan et al. 2009). The three basic postulates of this theory that also apply to phenomenology and ethnomethodology state that:

- Human beings act toward things based on the meanings that things have for them.
- The attribution of meaning to objects through symbols is a continuous process.
- The process takes place in a social context.

Symbolic interactionists have varied points of view. However, self-congruity, individual opinion, and empathy are the key subjects of symbolic interaction among the participants (Stryker and Vryan 2003). It also includes the interpretation of actions, because symbolic meanings may be derived differently. Elements such as social roles, traditional organizations, social and ethnic laws, and culture provide points of discussion to the individuals for forming definitions. In this context, symbolic interaction emphasizes social interaction, which forms the base of qualitative research. Two different thresholds, symbolism and interpretivism, in the society determine the features of symbolic interactionism that affect qualitative research. In symbolic interactionism, the process of conversation to acquire information is important. The responses of people in the society are affected by the knowledge ecosystem comprising self-learning, family, peer, and society. Knowledge and learning are affected also by the referred input.

Phenomenology

During the 20th century, phenomenology contributed in most areas of philosophy, including philosophy of mind, social philosophy, philosophical anthropology, aesthetics, ethics, philosophy of science, epistemology, theory of meaning, and formal ontology. It provided groundbreaking theoretical support for analyses of cognitive topics such as intentionality, embodiment, self-awareness, historicity, truth, evidence, perception, and interpretation (Zahavi 2008). The salient features of phenomenology are as discussed in the following:

- Phenomenologists try to use human thinking, intelligence, and perceptions to describe and understand human experiences.
- To understand the nature of human experience, we must study that experience, not an external world.
- Human experiences can be catalogued and described in order to create meaning. These appearances in the conscious mind are known as phenomena.
- Researchers try to identify the essential features of phenomena, and compare them with those described by other phenomenologists to identify features common to a population.
- Phenomenology suggests that people operate by assuming that others make the same kind of assumptions as they do about situations like "middle class kids," "working parents," and so on.

Phenomenology seeks to uncover a given phenomenon through people's experiences. Variation of conceptions related to a given phenomenon is defined as phenomenology. Phenomenology has achieved acceptance not only in philosophy, but also in anthropology, sociology, and psychology, and it has influenced the work of poets, artists, and novelists. Phenomenology and phenomenography describe the idea of Cartesianism, which is a variant appellation of positivism or rationalism. This school of thought assumes that knowledge should be acquired through the process of doubt, by making the self the absolute center of reality at the exclusion of human feelings, emotions, and opinions. Realistic phenomenology is an approach that requires the researcher to look into the real issues affecting people (Cibangu and Hepworth 2016). Phenomenology attempts to create conditions for the objective study of topics usually regarded as subjective. Consciousness, and the content of conscious experiences such as judgments, perceptions, and emotions are logically studied and expressed in phenomenology. Although phenomenology seeks to be scientific, it does not attempt to study consciousness from the perspective of clinical psychology or neurology. Instead, it seeks through systematic reflection to determine the essential properties and structures of experience of people. The qualitative research in social and cultural disciplines is, therefore, appropriately adapted to the phenomenological attributes, and is considered as one of the principal approached embedded in the qualitative inquiries.

The phenomenological concepts are well embedded within the consumer-centric companies to learn through consumer experiences, and use experiential marketing strategies to acquire new consumers. Disney portfolios are developed and improved through continuous qualitative research to document the phenomenological attributes of children, parents, and tour managers. The company studied what customers actually did in the park, using both ethnographic interviews and quantitative tools such as mapping family journeys around the park. It built a "garage," called the ideation lab, to prototype the "MagicBand," a digital device that it thought could solve the existing problems related to consumers' convenience. In 2014, Disney World rolled out the MagicBand across the park (Sheppard, Edson, and Kouyoumjian 2017).

Ethnography

Ethnography is the systematic study of people and their associated cultures. It explores cultural phenomena allowing the researcher to observe holistic perspectives of the society from the point of view of its sustained evolution, causes and effects, and behavioral complexities. Ethnography is a research tool used in anthropological research, which helps in exploring human culture, traditions, rituals, signs, symbols and behavior. Ethnography encourages researchers to observe, examine, and reflect upon the subjects during the course of research study. Conceptualizing ethnography as a research tool is a relative ontology, which applies to traditional research. Ethnographer examines the social, political, cultural, situational, personal, historical, and environmental conditions of subjects in the study (Brennan, Fry, and Previte 2015). In ethnography, researcher and subjects are integrally engaged to share their views on the predetermined topic. Data in the ethnographic tradition, therefore, contribute to continuous learning from the respondents. It can be subjective or objective, and may be intensely personal such as sharing reflexivity or distantly epiphenomenal. Epiphenomenalism is a philosophical state of mind in which cognitive process is affected by the changes in the physical states (Denzin 2011). The epiphenomenal research studies the convergence of mental life that affects physical dynamics or body reflexes within the social and personal surrounding. Accordingly, epiphenomenalism is a part of ethnographic research, and can be described as neurophysiological changes in the brain caused by events, retrieval of memory, or induced state of mind. Researchers acquiring qualitative information can be benefitted by the epiphenomenal observations of subjects during the study (Birnbacher 2006).

There are two types of ethnographic approaches: visual and documentary. Visual ethnography is about the collection of visual artifacts to the ethnographic record such as photographs, videos, maps, and clips, which are often complementary to auditory or documentary forms of data (Schwartz 1989). In the era of advanced information technology, the ethnographic research has evolved from face-to-face research to the use of digital platforms. It is widely accepted that respondents make little distinction between their online and offline personality, and people regularly share personal content and experiences via branded digital platforms like Facebook, Twitter, and Pinterest. The virtual platforms such as blogs and vlogs have also become the major resources of ethnographic text mining and virtual interactions. Digital platforms have become the new field for qualitative inquiry and have emerged as rich assets for carrying out participatory behaviors that unveil information about interesting lifestyle of people, and deliver information about emerging subcultural in contemporary society.

Growing new technologies have driven customers to become cocreators in developing customized products and services. New technologies have also allowed customers to disseminate personalized messages they receive, and authorize companies to customize the messages they would like to deliver in the society. Such services were once offered only to the elite for a very high cost, but application of technology by the companies for penetrating the mass market makes such customization much cheaper and easier. From jeans to coffee, to bicycles, to eyewear, to cosmetics, to vitamins, to breakfast cereals, companies have used this technology to create customized offerings. Managers have realized over time that if customers could get exactly what they want, they would not settle for some less-than-perfect standardized offering or message; and if companies could manufacture to order, the inventory reduction would go directly to the bottom line. Many firms focus on convergence of technology with customer value in promoting products and services in the mass markets. Realizing that firms, technology, and society had to coexist, companies, social networks, and social organizations look for ways to influence each other through joint social responsibility projects. This paves the way for the get-into-business stage, in which social networks and companies seek to serve the customers at bottom of the pyramid market segment by setting up successful businesses. In this process, customer learn through peers, while corporations gain an appreciation for the local knowledge, low-cost business models, and community-based marketing techniques. Increased success on both sides has laid the foundation for the co-created business in which companies and social networks become key parts of each other's capacity to deliver value (Burgmann and Prahalad 2007; Rajagopal 2013).

Social media has increasingly drawn more attention of consumers and companies over the traditional media. Accordingly, most companies have redefined the key factors of their marketing mix by reviewing the shifts in the consumer behavior, and online word of mouth competing for innovations in the products, operations, and services strategies. Many companies consider staying active in social media as a viable alternative to traditional advertising and communication. However, managers should understand that both traditional and online social media should serve as complementary to each other rather than relying on either one of them. A comparison of advertising and word of mouth shows that social media follow rules that are very different from traditional advertising. Social media can start conversations or build brand recognition, but the results are much more difficult to predict or measure (Armelini and Villanueva 2011). While working with social media, some companies have realized that the problem-solving process begins with the identification of exchange content and goals such as what does the customer need, and how does the company deliver solutions to meet those needs. The company's high degree of specialization may not be often ready to meet the shifts in the consumer behavior, as online interactive media drive the perceptions and attitudes of consumers faster than the traditional communications (Tuli et al. 2007).

Ethnographic research involves a prolonged, intensive, and direct involvement of the researcher in the lives and activities of people in the society. It is often used in conjunction with other terms such as participants' observation, qualitative methodology, a narrative case study, or social research. This methodology uses documents, observation, and interviewing people within a wide range of situations and contexts. Ethnography focuses on both the micro and macro aspects of society. The broad attributes of ethnographic research are as listed as follows:

- Production of a cultural knowledge of a group
- Description of activities from the point of view of members of the group
- Description of the characteristic features of group culture
- Description and analysis of patterns of social interaction
- Opportunity to document the insider opinions on the research theme, and
- Development of grounded theory based on the preliminary ethnographic inquiry

A researcher should stay with the subject, interact with them, and observe the psychosocial, cultural, and emotional attributes of the subjects to conduct the ethnographic research successfully. Most ethnographic researchers and journalists have spent months with lesser known tribes, villagers deprived of basic needs, and with the people at postdisaster rehabilitation camps to document their living conditions, expressions, and emotions. Under such conditions, a researcher must be both a member of the group and a stranger. During the research process, a level of cultural strangeness must be established and maintained. Most researchers begin as participant observers and end as informal interviewers.

Impact of Culture

Culture refers to the distinctive way of life of a group of people, their complete "design for a living." For ethnologists, folklorists, anthropological linguists, archaeologists, and social anthropologists, culture is always a point of departure or a point of reference, if not, invariably, the point of emphasis (Kluckhohn 1951). Culture consists of patterns, explicit and implicit of and for behavior acquired and transmitted by symbols, constituting the distinctive achievement of human groups, including their embodiment in artifacts. The core of culture consists of traditional concepts and values attached to it (Balazs 2002). The influence of cultural values on business negotiations have been diagnosed by Geert Hofstede (1991) by conducting research in 66 countries to measure the cross-cultural impact. The four cultural dimensions observed by Hofstede include individualism, which focuses on self-reference criterion, power distance index that leads to authority orientation, uncertainty index, which refers to the attitude of risk avoidance, and Masculinity/Femininity Index that tends to focus on assertiveness and achievements. Human value system is a synergy of societal values, family values, and individual values. Personality traits are largely evolved through family value and societal values that govern the family value paradigm. Such process is described as a pyramidal paradigm of personality and values, which has a large base of societal culture in the bottom of the pyramid, groomed into the family values, and ultimately shaping the personality at the top of the paradigm (Rajagopal 2004). Personality of an individual matters for gaining confidence within, and facing the extrinsic environment. Personality traits are largely groomed through the cultural settings observed in the native education, etiquette, language, expression ability, family, and friends. Native environment is also an important factor influencing the personality traits of a person (Onedo 1991). When a person cannot appraise his personality to the best of his satisfaction, he finds it difficult to get adjusted with the new culture and may like to confine to his native culture.

Companies learn consumer culture and develop products of pro-consumer demand by interacting with the consumers through researchers, salespeople, or engaging marketing research organizations to analyze the cognitive dimensions of consumers. Mattel Toys Inc., the creator of Barbie doll has adopted the approach to learn about the feelings of young girls on Barbie as their emotional friend. Barbie doll is a nonexpressive and silent, but an emotional object that reaches out through her physical attributes like clothing, facial expressions, and the still body language. The company learns through the consumer interface, focus group studies, and consumer videos about the next-generation Barbie. The significance of qualitative research in business and marketing is thus deeply rooted alongside the quantitative research practices.

Summary

Qualitative research is an effective tool to measure human values, emotions, and logical narratives through symbolic interactions, and ethnographic and phenomenological expedition. It offers an exciting experience to interact with the subjects, understand their perceptions, and draw relevant observations. Qualitative research needs an informal setting comfortable to the respondents and researcher that could create both privacy and confidence. It involves an interpretive, naturalistic approach to explore the research themes. Qualitative research is a flexible process, which allows researcher to modify the existing research propositions and formulate new dimensions of the study based on interpersonal information and observations. A good researcher develops semantics map on the interconnecting words outgrowing from the responses during the in-depth interviews in the qualitative research process. Qualitative researchers develop grounded theory and establish research propositions through meta-synthesis of the study by integrating relevant qualitative analytics. Interception and mediation in qualitative inquiries are considered as good attributes and are used on need basis. The ecosystem of qualitative research embeds grounded theory, and sociocultural and political environment at the background, while the research setting, development of research instrument, quality of information, arguments and validations, audiovisual aides, and the observation of researcher form the foreground of research. The qualitative research encourages explorative instead of experimental design of study, unlike quantitative research that uses random sampling within the specified criteria for the subjects like age, gender, education, income, and occupation. Fundamentally, a good qualitative research design includes objectives of the research, conceptual framework, research questions, data collection tools, and validation and interpretations of the contents Collecting information through in-depth interviews is followed as the principal technique to explore various perspectives from the subjects on a given theme or topic of research. The qualitative research has been evolved around school of thoughts led by positivism, empiricism, and interpretivism. The major methodologies in the qualitative research include symbolic interactions, ethnography, and phenomenology.

References

Aksan, N., B. Kisac, M. Aydin, and S. Demirbuken. 2009. "Symbolic Interaction Theory." *Procedia-Social and Behavioral Sciences* 1, no. 1, pp. 902–04.

Armelini, G., and J. Villanueva. 2011. "Adding Social Media to the Marketing Mix." *IESE Insight* 9, pp. 29–36.

Berg, B.L., and H. Lune. 2004. *Qualitative Research Methods for the Social Sciences*, vols. 5, Boston: Pearson.

Brennan, L., M.L. Fry, and J. Previte. 2015. "Strengthening Social Marketing Research: Harnessing "Insight" Through Ethnography." *Australasian Marketing Journal* 23, no. 4, pp. 286–93.

Birnbacher, D. 2006. "Causal Interpretations of Correlations Between Neural and Conscious Events." *Journal of Consciousness Studies* 13, nos. 1–2, pp. 115–28.

Burgmann, J., and C.K. Prahalad. 2007. "Co-creating Business's New Social Compact." *Harvard Business Review* 85, no. 2, pp. 80–90.

Cibangu, S.K., and N. Hepworth. 2016. "The Uses of Phenomenology and Phenomenography: A Critical Review." *Library & Information Science Research* 38, no. 2, pp. 148–60.

Chalmers A.G. 1982. *What is this Thing Called Science?* Queensland, Australia: University of Queensland Press.

Charmaz, K. 1995. "Grounded Theory." In *Rethinking Methods in Psychology*, eds. J. A. Smith, R. Harré, and L.V. Langenhove, 27–49. London: Sage.

Chaix, E., L. Deléger, R. Bossy, and C. Nédellec. 2018. "Text Mining Tools for Extracting Information About Microbial Biodiversity in Food." *Food Microbiology*, in press doi.org/10.1016/j.fm.2018.04.011

Chater, N., and M. Oaksford. 2000. "The Rational Analysis of Mind and Behavior." *Synthese* 122, nos. 1–2, pp. 93–131.

Denzin, N.K. 2011. "The Politics of Evidence." In *The SAGE Handbook of Qualitative Research*, eds. N.K. Denzin and Y.S. Lincoln, vols. IV, 645–57. Thousand Oaks, CA: Sage.

Fletcher, D., A.D. Massis, and M. Nordqvist. 2016. "Qualitative Research Practices and Family Business Scholarship: A Review and Future Research Agenda." *Journal of Family Business Strategy* 7, no. 1, pp. 8–25.

Hill, L.H. 2007. "Thoughts for Students Considering Becoming Qualitative Researchers—Qualities of Qualitative Researchers." *Qualitative Research Journal* 7, no. 1, pp. 26–31.

Kawulich, B.B. 2005. "Participant Observation as a Data Collection Method." *Forum: Qualitative Social Research* 6, no. 2, p. Art 43.

Langer, E., and A. Beard. 2014. "Mindfulness in the Age of Complexity." *Harvard Business Review* 92, no. 4, pp. 68–73.

Layder, D. 1994. *Understanding Social Theory*. London: Sage.

Mason. J. 2002. *Qualitative Researching*. London: Sage.

Ogbo, A., and A.A. Kifordu. 2015. "Diversity Management Research (DMR) as a Strategy for Sustainable Development in the Third World: Experiences and Future Plans of Intellectuals." *Procedia—Social and Behavioral Sciences* 195, pp. 1303–10.

Outhwaite, R.W. 2015. "Positivism, Sociological." In *International Encyclopedia of the Social & Behavioral Sciences*, ed. J.D. Wright, 2nd ed, 625–29. Amsterdam: Elsevier.

Rajagopal, A. 2017. "Epistemological Perspectives in Business Research: An Analytical Review." *International Journal of Business Competition and Growth* 6, no. 1, pp. 47–59.

Rajagopal, A. 2018. *Marketing Research: Fundamentals, Process, and Implications*. Hauppauge, New York, NY: Nova Publishers.

Rips, L.J. 2002. "Circular Reasoning." *Cognitive Science* 26, no. 6, pp. 767–95.

Ritchie, J., J. Lewis, C.M. Nicholls, and R. Ormston. 2013. *Qualitative Research Practice: A Guide for Social Science Students and Researchers*. London: Sage.

Russell-Rose, T., J. Chamberlain, and L. Azzopardi. 2018. "Information Retrieval in the Workplace: A Comparison of Professional Search Practices." *Information Processing & Management* 54, no. 6, pp. 1042–57.

Seale, C., G. Gobo, J.F. Gubrium, and D. Silverman. 2007. *Qualitative Research Practice*. London: Sage.

Sheppard, B., J. Edson, and G. Kouyoumjian. 2017. *More than a Feeling: Ten Design Practices to Deliver Business Value*. New York, NY: McKinsey & Co.

Stryker, S., and K.D. Vryan. 2003. "The Symbolic Interactionist Frame." In *Handbook of Social Psychology*, ed. J.D. Delamater. New York, NY: Springer.

Toplak, M.E., R.F. West, and K.E. Stanovich. 2014. "Rational Thinking and Cognitive Sophistication: Development, Cognitive Abilities, and Thinking Dispositions." *Development Psychology* 50, no. 4, pp. 1037–48.

Tuli, K.R., A.K. Kohli, and S.G. Bharadwaj. 2007. "Rethinking Customer Solutions: From Product Bundles to Relational Processes." *Journal of Marketing* 71, no. 3, pp. 1–17.

Zahavi, D. 2008. "Phenomenology." In *Routledge Companion to Twentieth-Century Philosophy*, ed. D. Moran. Philadelphia, PA: Routledge.

CHAPTER 2

Qualitative Research Design

Overview

Each qualitative research has an exclusive design for each occasion. It can be developed for longitudinal (temporal) and spatial studies. Longitudinal qualitative research design is used to study people or subjects of the same region over time in periodical intervals. Some ethnographic studies are longitudinal as the subjects are involved in comprehensive inquiries over time. This chapter addresses various aspects of qualitative research from defining problems to deriving synthesis. In qualitative inquiries, a researcher can choose broad community- or niche-oriented problems. Therefore, the roadmap of qualitative research discussed in this chapter offers guidance on the right perspective in defining research problems and elaborates on approaches to explore them. It is argued in this chapter that the qualitative research is the best-fit methodology to understand the perceptions of people in the cognitive, socio-cultural, and politico-economic domains. Thus, a significant discussion is focused on exploring the scope of qualitative research and developing the right research questions. The discussion on nine major hybrid insights on conducting the qualitative research provides rich information for researchers. Thoughts on developing research instrument for qualitative research and drawing synthesis on cognitive analytics of qualitative information further add value to this chapter.

Introduction

Qualitative research design is a flexible approach unlike the quantitative methodology. Research topics in qualitative inquiry determine the pattern of study design. Sampling, tools and techniques of data collection, dimensions of cognitive analytics, and data validation process are decided accordingly to develop the research design in qualitative research. Grounded theory is central to the design of qualitative research. The process of developing research design spans across descriptive examinations of research needs, its ecosystem, and prescriptive propositions of the research. Research design in qualitative research is developed through rigorous thinking and reasoning on the elements of research ecosystem. Sometimes, an asymmetrical relationship between the researcher and the subjects affects the predetermined research design and requires changes in the design mid-way into the research process. Due to the inductive attributes of research, developing research design around the theoretical frameworks is not a challenge in qualitative research; however, the rationale of grounded theory does influence the research design in qualitative inquiries (Cash 2018).

In conducting qualitative inquiries, the effectiveness of research depends on researcher–subject compatibility in the context of sociocultural, ethnic, economic, educational, and rational problems in the inquiry process. These interface and acquaintance factors need to be integrated in the research with proposed design of the study. The biggest challenge in qualitative research is the incompatibility between the applied management practices and the existing situations in the field. With the rise of multifaceted social projects, the need to develop research designs specific to the topics becomes imperative in qualitative methodologies. The research designs in qualitative research are knitted around five Ws comprising what, when, why, who, and where factors within the psychosocial and cognitive analytics. The research designs based on the ethnographic, phenomenological, and symbolic interactionism are founded within the epistemological assumptions of design research (Murphy 2017).

The qualitative researcher is the key player in the research design process, who continually deploys reflexivity and evaluative skills to develop an instrument for data collection and determines the information acquisition process. The researcher commands analysis and the decisions concerning the direction of the next step in the study. The design of each qualitative research study, therefore, is considered as unique for each occasion. Research designs in qualitative research can be developed for longitudinal (temporal) and spatial studies. Some ethnographic studies are longitudinal as the subjects are involved in comprehensive inquiries over time.

Studies analyzing socioeconomic development and quality of life of the subjects in a given region are planned over time intervals to measure the change. Methodological continuity and on-field situations suggest that research designs in qualitative research can be developed by establishing appropriate study goals and data requirements for both longitudinal and spatial studies. Sometimes, research deigns are subjected to subtle and minor methodological changes such as changes in subject identification approaches or revisions of interview questions. In other contexts, methodological modifications can lead to major changes, including additional data collection points, construction of additional interview protocols, or alternative data analysis approaches. Such designs are known as transitory study designs in qualitative research. From a methodological perspective, longitudinal qualitative research creates challenges in continuity of research, and is often accompanied by ethical dilemmas and confidentiality considerations from prolonged engagement with participants (Koro-Ljungberg and Bussing 2013).

The rationale and construction of qualitative research problems, questions, sampling strategies, data collection techniques, data analysis approaches, and interpersonal perspective of qualitative inquiries constitute the integrity of qualitative research designs. A widely recognized research design of qualitative inquiry is developed by making assumptions about the relationship between researchers and the subjects, the role of conceptual or theoretical paradigms, and the ways in which questions are asked. The research design is defined also as the approach to sampling or data collection, the analysis process, and the timeframe for qualitative study. The research design in qualitative research should be developed specific to the ethnography, phenomenological research, and narrative inquiries (Knapp 2017).

In theoretical qualitative research design, emotions also stimulate investigators to work with lead participants to engage in open-ended dialogues for acquiring information. A humanistic research design for qualitative research can be developed in the following manner (Wong et al. 2017):

- Researchers identify the need for an exploratory approach and potential to enrich data through priming the participants for in-depth inquiries.

- The data sampling and data collection tools are carefully developed considering technology tools.
- Relevant research questions are developed to optimize the information acquisition.
- Finally, data analysis is planned for the acquired information.

The design for qualitative research in marketing is widely used to understand consumer emotions, their perceived value on products and services, and interactivity on social media. Qualitative research is used by marketing research organizations and companies to understand, identify, and leverage the particular emotions, motivations, and self-image stimuli to maximize their competitive advantage and growth. In such qualitative research, companies perform cognitive analytics by bridging the market trend and customer insight data and develop qualitative descriptions of the elements that motivate their customers. These elements may be desire for freedom, security, perceived value, social status, and the like. Customer-centric companies analyze their customers to learn the stimuli and motivators important to the high-value group, which could help customers in developing a strong association with their brand. Such qualitative research provides a guide to the emotions they need to connect with, in order to create their most valuable customer segment (Magids, Zorfas, and Leemon 2015).

Qualitative research designs help companies explore six universal emotions that a common consumer feels, but does not commonly reveal, to the manufacturers and marketers. The sequential qualitative inquiries with consumers help the companies understand their happiness, anger, disgust, sadness, fear, and surprise about the products and services. The low-cost airlines, upon conducting qualitative surveys of air travelers in the airports and through the travel agencies, learn about consumer emotions and focus their marketing strategies on the consumer touch points. The Indian sky is getting congested with the low-cost and third-tier airlines, which are focusing on price and promotion strategies as critical touch points. Low-cost carriers like Indigo, Spice Jet, and Air Odisha are pursuing a "red ocean" strategy as they look to offer the lowest prices at a low cost. In Europe, Ryan Air, an Irish aviation company, has emerged as one of the strongest low-cost competitor within the airlines industry. Upon conducting casual interviews with young tourists across destinations, Ryan Air, for instance, was likely to introduce "standing only" or vertical seats while charging passengers between four to eight pounds per person, depending on the journey. However, the aviation regulatory authorities did not approve the proposal. The qualitative research thus helps companies develop out-of-the-box strategies based on analyzing consumer opinions. Smaller sized airlines with limited capital are likely to struggle increasingly in this environment against the strength of bigger players.

Qualitative Research: The Roadmap

The roadmap of qualitative research begins with the identification of an appropriate research problem, which is suited to the qualitative research design. The human elements in business like perception, value, leadership, governance, efficiency, and so on, underpin the relevant problems and raise opportunity for qualitative research. A right research problem help a researcher to develop a functional research design for qualitative inquiry. Decision-making in business needs analytics beyond data sets, which is usually supported by the qualitative information, and validation though the qualitative analysis might entail the risk inaccurate observation. In order to increase the chance of success, qualitative research is conducted on the behavior of consumers, managers, motivators, and other market role-players. Their responses and psychophysical actions and opinions are used to interpret the current situation and exploring the possible solutions. Therefore, it can be stressed that to develop an appropriate research design, it is necessary to identify a right research problem (Szyjewska-Bagińska and Szyjewski 2018). The stages of qualitative research are as discussed as follows:

- Defining the problem
- Developing an approach to the problem
  - Selecting type of study: exploratory, descriptive, experimental, casual
  - Developing research questions: proposition
- Formulating a research design

- ○ Sampling
- ○ Data collection
- ○ Scenario setting
- • Theoretical motivation
- • Methodology: study design
  - ○ Sampling, identifying variables, data collection, structuring constructs, research proposition(s)
  - ○ Quality assurance criteria
- • Instrument development
  - ○ Structured or semistructured, type of questions, core-peripheral-intercept questions
- • Preparing data sets, organizing data, coding, and analyzing data
- • Drawing inferences, presentation of results, and judgments on propositions
- • Implications, conclusions, and future research prospects

Qualitative researchers tend to choose convenience sample that can be as low as one subject. In this research process, information is acquired using interview technique, and drawing inference based on various perspectives of the subject. Designing research instrument is a lengthy process in qualitative research as it is refined many times in view of the interactions and the required interview protocols. Therefore, interviews are designed to generate the perspectives of subjects about their ideas, opinions, and experiences. In qualitative inquiries, a variety of methods of observation including taking general notes, using checklists or time-and-motion logs may be used. The transcription of information takes a long time, which deters many researchers from using this method.

Defining Research Problems

Problems for qualitative research can be defined from the existing research domain in the context of society. The broad and narrow spectra of problems can be mapped by the researcher to choose an appropriate problem. The spectrum of probable problems in the business and society are explained in Figure 2.1.

Figure 2.1 illustrates five domain of research areas for qualitative research with various broad and narrow spectrum problems. These research domains are contextual to business and society. Qualitative research is widely conducted to understand the perceptions of people in cognitive, sociocultural, and politico-economic domains. However, qualitative research also focuses on organizational problems to learn about employee behavior at various organizational tiers. Generation gap in the society has widened over time, and new generations have branched out paralleling growth in innovation and technology in the global marketplace. Thus, the qualitative research has also extended inquiries into the behavioral elements of generation-X, generation-Y, and millennial consumers. The generation-X consumers are those born during 1965 to 1975, while the generation-Y consumers are those aged 14 to 31 years in 2008, who are in the marketplace with the numbers and the purchasing power to have an unprecedented impact on the economy (Noble, Haytko, and Phillips 2009).

Cognitive inquiries using the qualitative research designs are commonly aimed at understanding the personality and behavioral issues of people (civil or defense) and consumers within the social and business contexts. Spatial and temporal research designs in qualitative inquiries are employed to measure stakeholder perceptions toward social development, quality of life, gender empowerment, and cultural perspectives in various geo-demographic segments. The social problems studied in qualitative research spread across education, health, housing, employment, and social infrastructure. In business, qualitative research is commonly applied to explore workplace culture, employee engagement, welfare measures, and performance of corporate social responsibility. Besides these problem areas, corporate relations, role of government, and public relations also form the core of qualitative research problems. On the politico-economic platform, discussions on political ideologies, public participation, impact of economic policies on quality of life, and critical views of citizens constitute the core issues for research using qualitative methodology. Social entrepreneurship and social innovation research have emerged as new areas of qualitative research, which focus on analyzing the information about challenges of designing hybrid society. Such socioeconomic development integrates the competing institutions to tackle social problems

Narrow spectrum of research problems

Personality
Expectations
Emotions
Anthropomorphic
Motivation
Behavioral

Governance
Empowerment
Quality of life
Cultural distortion
Social development
Social needs
Social change

Growth
Welfare of employees
Goals and process
Employee engagement
Workplace culture

Individual values
Spatial and temporal lessons
Concerns and views
Public participation
Political manifesto
Economy, inequality, and gaps
Quality of life

Self-esteem
Quality and value
Adoptability
Inquisitiveness

Cognitive

Socio-cultural

Organizational

Politico-economic

Technological

People
Consumers
Business
Society

Knowledge management
Social innovation
Public policies
Development perspectives

Government
Public relations
Corporate policies

Political ideology
International influence
Economic development
Public economy
Industrial policies

Economy of scale
Productivity and quality
Innovation
Technology growth

Broad spectrum of research problems

Research domains

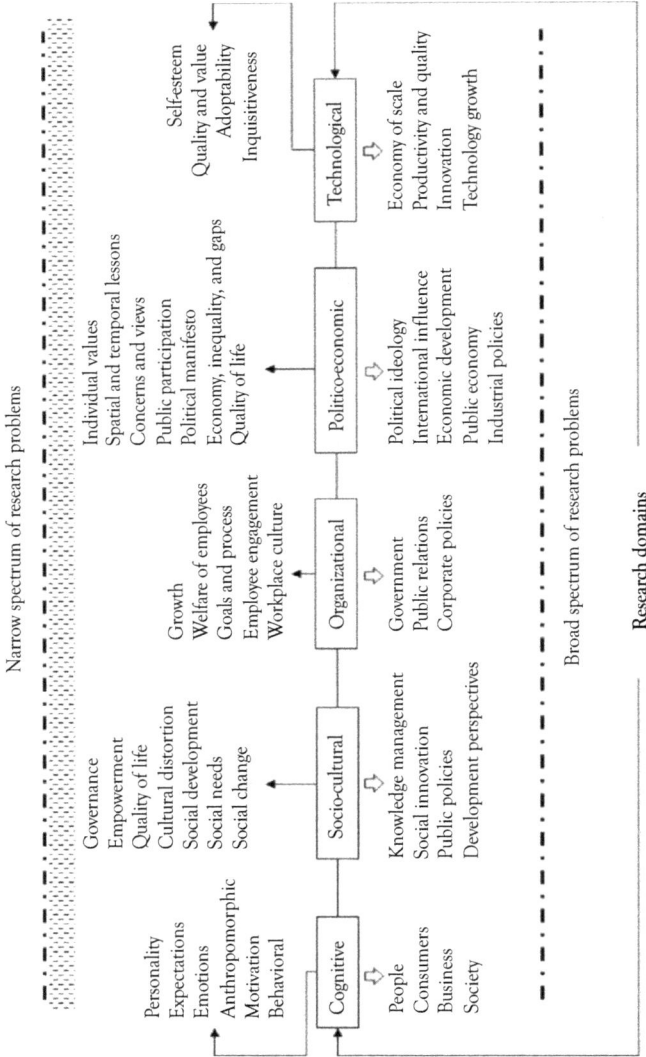

Figure 2.1 *Mapping research problems*

using market-based methods, especially in developing economies that can be studied spatially and longitudinally through the qualitative research designs.

Approach to Study Research Problems

Upon defining the problem for qualitative research, the type of research to be conducted is decided. The researchers choose one of the two common types of research designs—exploratory or experimental, which can fit into the qualitative research methodologies. *Exploratory research design* is used to study a research problem by obtaining comprehensive information. This research design is chosen when there is a paucity of studies on the problem and inadequate evidence exists to predict an outcome. The focus of exploratory research design is to gain prima facie insights and familiarity on the identified problems. Exploratory designs are often used as gateways to advance in studying an issue, and to determine what methodology would effectively help in collecting quality information about the issue. Exploratory study designs develop familiarity with basic details, settings, and concerns, and deliver a well-acquainted picture of the research environment. This approach helps in developing new ideas and assumptions to derive new concepts and grounded theory to guide qualitative research or propositions. In this study design, the predetermined research problems are refined for more systematic investigation and formulation of new research questions. Exploratory research generally utilizes small sample sizes; hence, findings are not generalizable to a large population. In exploratory research design, a researcher can gain insights on the behavioral and environmental issues but cannot derive definitive conclusions. This research design is flexible and often unstructured, leading to opinion analytics and tentative conclusions that have limited value to decision-makers. Often, the research norms and ethics applied to qualitative methods are subjective to respondents and researchers for information acquisition.

Experimental research design allows the researcher to acquire opinion of subjects on a theme, dividing them into the control and non-control groups. Control group subjects are those who have experienced the benefits of a given cause like using the entrepreneurial loans or are involved in a process like social development. The subjects of noncontrol group are observers, gatekeepers, and influencers within the aforementioned environment. This research design is often used where there is causal relationship (cause precedes effect) and consistency in a causal relationship (a cause will always lead to the same effect) with high proximity value. The classic experimental design specifies an experimental group and a control group. The independent variable is administered to the experimental group, not to the control group; and both groups are measured on the same dependent variable. The effective experimental research should be conducted with control, randomization, and marginal manipulation. Most researchers in social sciences seek causal explanations that need enormous information for validating the propositions in the qualitative research.

Most pharmaceutical companies conduct clinical trials on new medicinal formulas by carrying out in-depth inquiries with the patients who form the control group. The Pfizer Clinical Research Unit (CRU) in New Haven, Connecticut, provides comprehensive clinical care and monitors clinical trial volunteers during their stay at the unit. The CRU is engaged in conducting a study of a marketed prescription drug that has been in the market since 2016 for curing mild to moderate atopic dermatitis. The research is likely to employ experimental research with qualitative research attributes.

Causal effect (nomothetic perspective) occurs when variation in one phenomenon affects the variables in another related phenomenon. For example, in social development research, improvement in the educational facilities in less developed demographics affects the quality of life and social value in the society. Nomothetic perspective is known as "trait" approach,' used to study and predict behavior in a given situation. Psychologists adopting this approach hold that traits are source of human personality. A trait is assumed to be any enduring characteristic of an individual, which is relatively stable and influences human behavior. Qualitative researchers use nomothetic approach combined with observations during the in-depth interviews or participatory research appraisals to measure the personality-related factors. Discussion on the prior attributes explains the *causal research design* used by the qualitative researchers.

Longitudinal qualitative research design is used to study people or subjects of the same region over time in periodical intervals. Such research design is managerially termed as *action research design*, which is generally applied for monitoring the socioeconomic development programs and their impact on social welfare and well-being of people. Such monitoring and measurement programs in qualitative research are conducted in "social laboratories," where researchers are engaged in conducting continuous interviews with people. Social laboratory is a collaborative venture among researchers, community, and local governing bodies, which encourages action research design for studying community situations. Action research design focuses on pragmatic and solution-driven outcomes rather than testing theories. Practitioners use action research, as it allows them to learn consciously from the experience of participants. Action research continuum can be regarded as a learning cycle. Action research studies lead to improving practice and advocating for change. They focus on the collaborative learning and the design, enactment and evaluation of liberating actions within social, cognitive, and anthropological areas. These studies offer action and reflection in an ongoing cycle of co-generative knowledge (Coghlan and Brydon-Miller 2014).

Qualitative research is often used in the health care research. The qualitative research designs are commonly applied to understand the values and perceptions of patients and clinical trial respondents, and social response to the community and social-preventive medicines. The health service researchers view qualitative research as a tool including focus groups, in-depth interviews, methods for developing consensus, and participants' observation, and so on. Accordingly, researchers develop grounded theory and initiate the process of qualitative inquiry. Researchers apply qualitative research methodologies to explore the sociocultural determinants of health. Within the community health sector, the cohort research design is used to explain the causes of disease by exploring how the human psycho-sociological factors interact with the disease agent and the environment. Disease prevention strategies generated from good qualitative research tend to be more effective, since they focus on the very core of unhealthy host behavior (Isaacs 2014).

Upon defining an appropriate research problem for qualitative research, the study area needs to be determined. However, in the reverse process, a study area is defined first, and the right research problem to be studied is explored later. For example, to study the socioeconomic development experience of the population in a less developed region, the study is defined first, and later a research problem is chosen rationally. The next step is to describe the topic of the research study to provide a contextual understanding and explain the significance of research topic in reference to studying the human experience. This is done by collecting demographic information, statistics, and trends. In addition, academic debates on the subject would enable the researchers to justify the thesis of the research appropriately and develop grounded theory. In this process, conventional wisdom of researchers and previously laid ideologies would also support the rationale of the qualitative research. Methodology for the qualitative inquiry can be created, refined, and applied to collect information in the next stage. It is also necessary to delineate whether the qualitative research is a case study, spatial investigation, or a longitudinal approach.

Research Questions and Propositions

Developing research questions is a sensitive task in qualitative research because the quality of information depends on the questions asked. Upon defining a research problem, the questions should be framed for understanding the ecosystem of the research problem. The ecosystem of a research problem consists of the following elements:

- Understanding problem: trigger questions
- Cause and effect: core questions
- Gravity of problem: intercept questions (social, cultural, ethnic, economic, political, technology, legal implications)
- Personality factors: questions related to self-congruency and cognition
- Remedial stances: questions concerning perceptions on possible solutions to the problem

The trigger questions should be broader in scope, while the succeeding questions on problem ecosystem can be proportionately narrowed in scope to focus on acquiring quality information. Research propositions in qualitative research are the arguments developed on the assumptions in the context of grounded theory. Several propositions can be developed in qualitative research, which need to be validated from the point of view of commonality and argumentative clarity. However, all proposition in qualitative research are contextual and in reference to the study area, sample population, and the assumptions made during the study. It is difficult to generalize the propositions developed during the study at a macro- or meso level. Propositions developed in the qualitative research should be contextual to the objectives of the research. Commonly, the propositions in qualitative research are developed considering the previous research studies and initial observations of the researchers during the pilot study or focus group.

Scope of Qualitative Research

Qualitative methods have a wide scope of use within socio-cultural, political, ethnic, economic welfare, human development, leadership, community health research, and clinical trials. They can address issues such as critical opinions, new ideas, informed consent, and randomized information, and allow respondents to share their own experiences of the benefits and impacts of various developmental perspectives. Beyond sharing personalized and community opinions of subjects, the ecosystem of the study enhances the scope of research in diversified and symbiotic themes such as technology and society, globalization and ethnicity, and political ideologies and human development. Often, respondents help researchers in drawing right inferences for complex, unclear, and induced responses. To date, qualitative methods have not been widely used in community health and clinical trials to evaluate the use of psychotropic drugs in older or younger people, or more specifically in people with dementia. Hence, there is wider scope of research in community health, social preventive medications, and clinical trials. The qualitative research is participatory, where subjects feel valued for their information. The participatory methodology encourages reflexive behavior among the subjects to share inside information, which could not be obtained through quantitative research (Gibson et al. 2004).

The scope of qualitative research spreads across cross-sectional studies that collect data from two or more sections of a sample, based on the geo-demographic differences within the target community. Like cross-sectional studies, longitudinal studies are also conducted with qualitative methodology, as they are concerned with factors affecting the change (Taguchi 2018). The extended scope of qualitative research covers the following areas of research on consumer behavior including the study of consumer perception to buying decisions:

- Consumer perceptions
- Media and communication models
- Relationship and convergence
- Customer value measurement
- Social networking models
- Asymmetric behavior model
- Buying decisions and factor sensitivity

Qualitative research is one of the dominant methodologies used to understand consumer perception in reference to the media, publicity, and referral programs. These studies measure the expectations and impact of consumers on products and services. The scope of qualitative methodologies is used to explore consumer relationship, social networking, and buying behavior. Documenting heterogeneous information, and drawing inferences on behavioral inputs in spatial and longitudinal studies can be well documented through qualitative studies.

Inductive reasoning enhances the scope of cognitive analytics with observation of specific instances and seeks to establish generalizations. Most often, qualitative research follows an inductive process. However, in most occurrences, the theory developed from qualitative investigation may not be able to validate the theory over the spatial and temporal dimensions. Qualitative researchers demonstrate deductive and inductive processes in their research but fail to recognize these processes. Adoption of formal deductive procedures can represent an important step for assuring consistency in qualitative research findings (Hyde 2000). However, the qualitative research methodology is blamed for subjectivity and biasness in drawing inferences and inductive observations. Developing good research ideas is both a science and an art. The researcher should develop knowledge on theoretical foundations and learn the ethical parameters on conducting qualitative research. Initially, as the researcher decides upon an approach to utilize in the research process, research directors and sponsors should encourage the researcher to develop research questions that would expand the knowledge on the topic of research and enhance the scope of information acquisition. In order to expand the research knowledge base, the research proposal should be meticulously reviewed and information should be acquired through the taxonomy of research questions (Bradley 2001; Rajagopal 2018).

Hybrid Insights

Identify

Qualitative research has evolved across epistemological discussions and research methodologies. However, one major challenge exists in the qualitative design toward the identification of right problem for the research. As qualitative inquiry moves around personality and sociocultural development, researchers need to exercise the problem diagnostics among subjects and within the study area. Accordingly, a specific problem is identified, which is later refined to match with the broad objectives of the study, and justified based on previous research studies, community concerns, and relevant public policies.

Define

The problem defined for qualitative research should be expounded in reference to corollaries among the research model, common sense, and the expected outcome of the study. The common sense of researchers in defining the problem for qualitative inquiries is a sensitive issue as it is often drifted by the community voice, project sponsoring organization, government, or self-image congruence. In defining a research problem, statements need to be avoided. However, the problem definition should be carefully structured without implicit meanings and wordiness. While explaining the research problems, it is necessary to specify whether the study discovers, seeks to understand, explores, or describes the experiences. However, prior to defining the problem, the social phenomenon to be researched should be seen as provisional and negotiated with consistent information. The objective of the study needs to be initially developed as provisional in the qualitative research, as it gets refined over time with the intercepting variables and the ecosystem of the problem. The objective of the study can be comprehensively defined after successfully completing the process of discovery of the problem and its justification. Research questions related to the specific problem should be explained without the use of non-directional wording in the question.

For example, to understand behavioral branding, it important to define cognitive dimensions of consumers on social and consumption brands. Behavioral branding is a cognitive approach of building brands, perceived by consumers as an integrated constituent of their desire and interest, and draws attention to derive satisfaction within the lifestyle and vogue. This is a well-knitted behavioral concept of consumers, which can be studied through the qualitative research. Cognitive branding suggests a pragmatic method, which can be termed as value profile, to ensure that such brands can influence consumer behavior by espousing social and cultural values. Behavioral branding thus becomes a catalyst for the emotional aspects associated with social, cultural, and ethical values of consumers, and a potential topic for qualitative research (Thellefsen et al. 2013).

Describe

The problem defined for the qualitative research can further be supported by socioeconomic, ethno-cultural, and cognitive semantics. Semantics is the linguistic and logical expression of the meaning of the research problem interrelated with a variety of variables determining causes and effects. The semantics can be predetermined, or formal semantics can be developed during the initial study process. The semantics of the problem describes logical aspects of derived meaning, such as sense, reference, implication, and logical form, to justify the research problem and choose appropriate study design. Qualitative researchers commonly organize focus group sessions with random subjects, or converse informally with target informants to explain the objectives of the research, and to acquire first hand opinion on the research problem.

The hybrid insights in the context of developing a research in qualitative research are shown in Figure 2.2.

All hybrid insights described in Figure 2.2 are discussed in this section. In qualitative inquiries, research designs are flexible and are revised depending on the problem ecosystem and attributes of the sample population for research in study area. As a large amount of verbal and nonverbal information is analyzed in the qualitative research, the content analysis need to be screened for removing the redundancy in information and involuntary biases.

Inspire

Qualitative researchers need to stimulate and inspire the subjects to share information, as people are often conservative and refrain from sharing information. In order to inspire the subjects, researchers need to exhibit socialization skills and generate confidence among the respondents. Ethnographic researchers stay with the target respondents for log time, mingle with them by participating in their social and cultural events, and become a family member. Such socialization behavior builds trust of a researcher within the geodemographic segment. Human relationship in qualitative inquiries serve as the gateway to quality information. Qualitative research often produces surprising and inspiring individual stories, storyboards (chain stories on any event or query), and cognitive portraits (individual experiences) that are invaluable for research designers. In this process, sometimes more rigor is needed to generate insights and streamline the thought process. Hybrid insights approach serves for both concept designing and developing business strategies by embedding individual stories into larger data sets. Since the qualitative research is a human-centered approach, search, observation, interviews, and other qualitative tools help in identifying latent or emerging consumer needs (Seemann 2012).

Explore

In a qualitative research perspective, a research study could attempt to explore behavioral branding in reference to co-creation and vogue

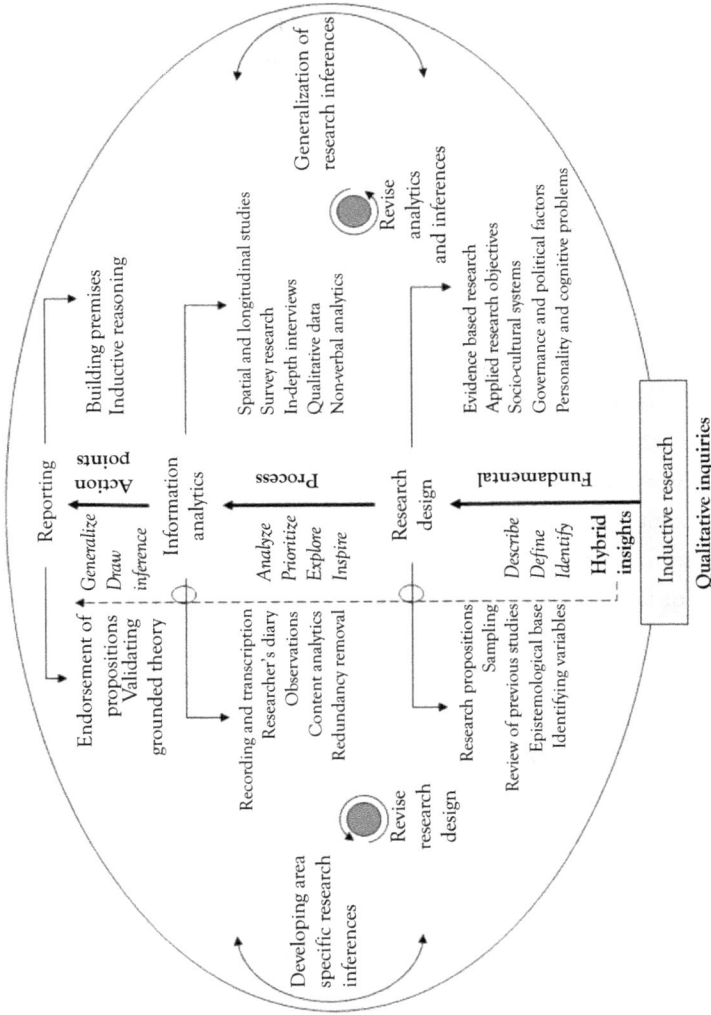

Figure 2.2 Hybrid insights and qualitative research design

dimensions. Branding behavior can be developed for establishing brand beliefs, evoking brand experience, developing trendy brands, sharing consumer experience, and building consumer behavior (Dev and Keller 2014). This stage focuses on the discovered needs, derived insights, and behavioral patterns for mapping the discussions. Researchers need to be alert in exploring information from the subjects as they may encounter provocations, implicit meanings, and undemocratic behavior among the sample population. Behavioral clusters can be introduced during the explore stage of research to set up detailed inquiry at mutual convenience.

The most effective way of acquiring qualitative information is by encouraging the subjects to speak liberally, rationally, and deliver interconnected contents during the interview process. Therefore, documenting uninterrupted narrations help researchers explore comprehensive information for the study. Narrative inquiry, a relatively consistent qualitative methodology, is the study of understanding the experience narratively. It is a way of thinking about, and studying, experience. Narrative inquiry follows a recursive, reflexive process of moving from field notes to field data to interim and final research reports. Alongside organizing the particular interviews, researchers may also like to document the random narrations on common social problems in public places. Narrative inquiry highlights ethical matters and shapes new theoretical understandings of people's experiences. Long narratives are classified as storytelling in qualitative inquiry. The storytelling may be autobiographical, biographical, testimonial, or personal experience. Thus, narrative is a spoken, written, or visual story that can be presented in various conversational formats serves by exploring the streamlined information.

Prioritize

In qualitative inquiries, information flow during the study is often enormous, unorganized, and raw. Therefore, all qualitative information needs to be scrutinized for consistency, quality, and validity. While classifying the qualitative information, the key indicators to the research proposition must be identified and arranged on priority for analytics. The data can be arranged in a two-dimensional matrix across information categories and sample clusters in the order of priority for content analysis.

Analyze

Data analysis in qualitative research broadly includes content analysis, observations, and written documents. Some critical aspects in data collection and management of information include resource use based on cost and time, quality of information, and using appropriate filters to prepare the data for analysis. Information analysis in qualitative research demands a robust content analysis. Some researchers also use descriptive statistics, if possible, while quantifying small qualitative samples. Graphic and pictorial illustrations are also extensively used in analyzing and reporting the findings of qualitative information. However, it is essential for researchers to check the consistency of findings with the predetermined propositions of the study. The use of information analytics techniques are classified as thematic listing of information, or content analysis of large and complex narrations. The information analytics process is built around common ideas from the data and does not necessarily require verbatim transcripts.

Recording the responses in electronic devices involves reduction in the original length of data documentation in the field. However, it is necessary to select the relevant data to be transcribed within the underlying assumptions of qualitative research design to carry out content analysis. Researchers should meticulously identify the conversations of the respondents that focus on divergent opinions and involve complex arguments for transcribing in parts. All necessary care must to be taken by the researchers while transcribing the recorded conversation, so the original contents would not be disrupted. Verbal and nonverbal interaction together need to be considered during the transcriptions to derive the right communicative meaning. Content analysis is an essential research technique to describe the qualitative information, narrations, and nonverbal illustrations of individuals, groups, and government programs in a field (Rajagopal 2018).

Observations during qualitative research comprise emotions and gestures of the subjects, and the social dynamics around. Social media websites provide a public forum that gives individual consumers the opportunity to present their observations, and access product information that facilitates their purchase decisions. User-generated online reviews on products and services proliferate among peer consumers through social media that drives a great impact on marketing (Trusov et al. 2010). The word-of-mouth, which percolates down the neighborhood, not only increases guiding messages for consumers, companies, and marketers toward converging better value chains, but also alters the processing of consumer information in building customer-centric marketing strategies. Peer communication through social media has emerged as a new form of consumer socialization, which is driving the consumer decision-making and helping companies to develop value-added marketing strategies (Casteleyn et al. 2009; Rajagopal 2018).

Drawing Inference

Contents of information acquired through qualitative research techniques should be analyzed categorizing the information and its fit to the research model. It should be determined whether analysis of the partial information or complete information is required to validate research propositions. Accordingly, inferences are drawn to support the results and conclusions considering the aspects of informants' experiences, opinions, and feelings. Drawing inferences in qualitative research is sensitive, as researchers are often influenced by subjectivity concerns and involuntary biasness. Cognitive bias is an involuntary pattern of thinking that leads to distorted perceptions and judgments that can result in errors in reasoning, logic, and evaluation. This is often a reason for people making suboptimal or irrational decisions (Kahneman and Tversky 1996). Due to repetition of information, drawing inferences by analyzing qualitative information is often complex. Qualitative research is documented in various ways, so the conclusions need to be streamlined. Making sense of the information begins as the first data are collected. Often, inferences in the qualitative research involves loop-like patterns as new connections in the data keep emerging while writing the report.

Generalize

Generalization of conclusions in the qualitative research is a difficult task. Since the opinions analyzed are based on the acquired information during the study and refer to a specific sociocultural, ethnic, cognitive ecosystem, it would be biased to generalize the conclusions at macro level. However, commonality in opinions can be established if the qualitative inquiries are spanned across the micro- and meso-regional divisions. Generalization is an act of reasoning, which involves drawing some broad inferences from particular observations or smaller study sample. It is widely acknowledged as a quality standard in quantitative research but is more controversial in qualitative research. The fundamental objective of qualitative studies is to provide a rich, contextualized understanding of psychosocial experience of population through the intensive study of particular cases, not to bring out a generalized decision.

In the research areas like social development, economic growth, entre-preneurial promotion, or personality improvement in the society, evi-dence-based research and qualitative opinions may lead to generalization of conclusions. The possibility of generalization in qualitative research can be considered in the context of classic sample-to-population general-ization (basic statistics), analytic generalization across the sample taxon-omy including geo-demographic segments, and case-to-case transference of conclusions (Polit and Beck 2010).

Pathway to Synthesis

Qualitative research design process has chronologically evolved across the epistemological philosophies, which helps researchers in developing syn-thesis with theoretical support. Researchers often lean toward a particular school of thought while reviewing the information draw inferences on the qualitative information. Research designs based on various epistemologies are as stated in the following:

- Epistemological: History of methods
  - Positivist approach
    - Qualitative, logical, perceptual narration Inductive
  - Interpretivism
    - Quantitative, evidence based
    - Pragmatic: Deductive
  - Triadic convergence
    - Theme, design, process

- ■ Illustrative, interpretive, impressionistic
- Problem-based research: Applied and real-time perceptions analysis by reviewing the causes and effects of previous projects
- Cross-sectional research designs and synthesis patterns
  - ○ Spatial and temporal
- Secondary qualitative research design and synthesis
  - ○ Published sources
  - ○ Text mining (digital)

Researchers with the positivist's theoretical motivation tend to pool information of the subjects and conduct analysis of data considering the quality of information, rationale and logic across the ideas, arguments, and criticism related to the key indicators of the study. This approach of analyzing data is widely based on cognitive and perceptual mapping, emerging semantics from the sequential arguments, and quality of narration. Positivist researchers believe in inductive research unlike those who follow quantitative, evidence-based, and pragmatic research design using the deductive analytics. Triadic convergence models in the qualitative research advocate blending research theme with the study design and the research process and make the data analysis more impressionistic through illustrative and interpretive abilities to discuss the study results. Problem-based qualitative research studies like psychosocial cognitive effects of relocated families due to implementation of mega developmental projects use applied and real-time perspectives of the subjects for analysis and synthesize the opinions in reference to the merits or demerits of previous practices. Cross-sectional studies in qualitative research are largely longitudinal in nature over space and time and cover the information on multiple sectors.

Qualitative research is also conducted using the secondary information acquired through published documents, pictures, and charts. As the information technology is growing rapidly over the years, digital platforms of companies, consumers, and social media networks have encouraged people to share their views liberally across the geo-demographic population. Most researchers today rely on "text data mining" by acquiring, pooling, and analyzing the information using these digital platforms. It is the process of deriving high-quality information from the text available on print or digital platforms. Since its emergence, text mining has involved multidisciplinary studies, focused primarily on database technology, web-based collaborative writing, text analysis, and machine learning for discovering new areas in knowledge management. The textual data sources for information extraction span across free-form text to semiformatted text (HTML, XML, and others digital formats). The data sources include the data pools encoded in open source document formats, data warehouses, and other proprietary formats. In the data-text-mining process, the keywords associated with the main labels such as knowledge discovery and text mining, can be categorized in reference to periods from 1998 to 2009. In addition to these terms, sentiment analysis, review manipulation, microblogging data, and knowledgeable users were the other terms frequently used from 2010 to 2017 (Usai et al. 2018).

Syntheses in qualitative inquiries are always debatable as they are intangible, being based on the opinions that cause subjectivity in drawing conclusions. Synthesis is the ultimate step in any ideology, epistemology, or qualitative information analytics. This can be achieved upon logically moving from the one-step to another, which begins from developing a thesis for qualitative research. The pathway to synthesis categorically consists of various stages as discussed in the following:

- Thesis
  - Identifying the research problem
  - Setting objectives
  - Conceptualization
  - Theoretical motivation
- Antithesis
  - Previous studies
  - Counterarguments
  - Logical framework analytics
- Hypothesis/proposition
  - Statement of propositions
  - Justification
  - Research model

- Synthesis
  - Content analysis
  - Meta-analysis
  - Meta-synthesis
  - Limitations and future research

Thesis

A thesis of a qualitative research emerges by determining a right question(s) on a right research problem. This logical process converges the research question and the problem to derive a thesis for conducting qualitative research. The reflective and interrogative processes required for developing effective qualitative research questions can help researchers in developing a good thesis and give shape and direction to a study. A thesis supported with the variables chosen from a wider ecosystem of research grows longitudinally over space and time in qualitative inquiries. However, good research questions do not always necessarily produce good research, but a rationally developed thesis might stay sustainable in all subsequent stages of a study (Agee 2009). In qualitative studies, the ongoing process of questioning often prompts researchers to revise the thesis of their research. Sometimes, the thesis in qualitative research is also formed collectively, where participants are invited to collaborate on the formulation of research questions, especially in participatory action research or in social laboratories. Such events call for a larger interactive process wherein the primary premises of qualitative inquiry are more fully realized (Stringer 2007). Developing thesis for qualitative investigation embeds the synchronization of tasks that include identifying research problem, setting objectives, conceptualization, and seeking theoretical motivation.

Conceptualization of a qualitative research model is the blueprint of research. It indicates the principal dimensions of the research and the variables responsible for measuring the cause and effect and exhibits interrelationship of research dimensions and variables with the research propositions. A conceptual framework represents the researcher's journey to explain a phenomenon. It maps out the actions required in the course of the study given his previous knowledge of other researchers' point of view and his observations on the subject of research.

Conceptualization reveals how particular variables in the study connect with each other. It is the process map to pursue the investigation.

The conceptual framework is worked out from the theoretical background and with the support of previous studies. The theoretical motivation draws support from time-tested theories that embody the findings of previous research studies on why and how a particular phenomenon occurs. For example, why consumer-spending declines on some occasions can be studied using qualitative methodology by developing a conceptual framework based on findings of the previous studies and theories of economic recession. Consumer spending usually falls in reference to rising prices and stagnation in the consumers' income. The data from credit card companies reflects that personal investment and value for money concerns of consumers affect their spending pattern. In view of such cause-and-effect situation, a researcher may like to develop the conceptual framework in relation to variables representing prices, income, value for money, and investment leading to a research proposition that states "consumer spending declines because of high price and low-income syndrome in the society."

Antithesis

Antithesis in qualitative inquiry is beyond the etymological sense of "juxtaposition" of a verbal argument. It refers to debate on research objectives, methodologies, and findings related to the topic of research. A research can array in a table the "for" and "against" arguments of the previous studies related to the topic of research and identify the gaps in both types of conversations across the spatial and temporal studies. The identified gap would provide opportunity to the researcher for strengthening the justification to conduct the study on the desired problem. Accordingly, qualitative researchers can thoroughly review the previous studies and develop counterarguments to fill the research gaps. In addition, logical framework analysis can be used to determine the justified path of research by observing the gaps in the previous studies. The logical framework approach (LFA) is a methodology mainly used for designing, monitoring, and evaluating development projects. It provides clear, concise, and systematic information about a research study through a process framework through linking goal, objectives, methodology, indicators, and results. The LFA helps in connecting these components in one framework, exhibiting their correlations and organizing the expected outcomes.

Setting qualitative research scenario is a challenging task for researchers in which research questions, propositions, and constructs of the study need to be developed upon reviewing the previous studies. It has been argued that a cross-cultural paradigm based on Markus and Kitayama's (1991) self-construal theory forms the basis for contemporary theoretical approach to the emerging field of qualitative research. Adopting this paradigm has led to some reservations about the helpfulness of sociocultural propositions for promoting theory development in this area. Most qualitative researches are inductive in nature and allow the researcher to generate research propositions from analyzing the collected data. The questions supporting the research propositions act as the distinguishing factors between qualitative research and quantitative research. With qualitative studies, research propositions are formed based on the research data and are developed to confirm or reject the preconceived notions, relationships, or correlations (Burck 2005).

Synthesis

Content analysis has three distinct approaches comprising conventional, directed, or summative. All three approaches are used to interpret meaning from the content of text data and, hence, adhere to the naturalistic paradigm. The major differences among the approaches are coding schemes, origins of codes, and threats to trustworthiness. In conventional content analysis, coding categories are derived directly from the text data. With a directed approach, analysis starts with a theory or relevant research findings as guidance for initial codes. A summative content analysis involves counting and comparisons, usually of keywords or content, followed by the interpretation of the underlying context (Hsieh and Shannon 2005).

Meta-analysis is the statistical procedure for combining data from multiple studies. When the treatment effect (or effect size) is consistent from one study to the next, meta-analysis can be used to identify this common effect. Decisions about the impact of an intervention or the validity of a proposition in qualitative research cannot be based on the information analytics of a case or narrow sample study, because the results may not fit to the generalization standards. Therefore, the mechanism of meta-analysis helps in synthesizing opinions across spatial studies. For example, a common social problem like "adolescents' behavior toward family in Western culture" can be studied across different states in a country, and meta-analysis can be used as methodology to earmark variations. The conclusion and action points may be generalized following the meta-analysis of qualitative inquiry accordingly. Narrative reviews could be used for this purpose. However, redundancy and biases should be removed from the narrative reviews to derive commonalities in the opinions across geo-demographic segments. Meta-analysis, by contrast, applies objective research frameworks and can be used with any number of studies.

In the health care segment, hospitals use meta-analysis through qualitative inquiries in reference to patients' behavior related to curative, preventive, and social medicines. They conduct series of studies in these research areas and draw categorical conclusions. In addition, pharmaceutical companies also use meta-analysis to gain approval for new drugs, with regulatory agencies sometimes requiring a meta-analysis as part of the approval process. Applied researchers in medicine, education, psychology, criminal justice, and a host of other fields also use meta-analysis to determine best possible preventive or developmental interventions. Meta-analysis is also widely used in basic research to evaluate the evidence in areas as diverse as sociology, social psychology, sex differences, finance and economics, political science, marketing, ecology, and genetics, among others.

Meta-synthesis is the systematic review and integration of findings from qualitative studies. It is an emerging technique in medical research that employs many different methods. Nevertheless, the method must be appropriate to the specific scientific field in which it is used. Meta-synthesis method has been adapted from thematic synthesis and phenomenology approaches to fit the particularities of psychiatric research. This method offers an appropriate balance between an objective framework, a rigorously scientific approach to data analysis, and the necessary contribution of the researcher's subjectivity in the construction of the final work. Qualitative syntheses refer to an integration of different methods for systematically reviewing and bridging the findings from sequential qualitative studies over space and time (Lachal et al. 2017).

Qualitative Research Instrument

Qualitative research questions are largely open-ended and provide ample space to the respondent to express. Most questions are of direct nature. However, information on some sensitive variables are sought using indirect questions. In a qualitative study, the researcher must develop research questions relevant to the propositions and objectives of the study. Research questions should be categorized as lead and supportive questions. Lead questions attribute to the core response related the study and are addressed directly to the respondents. The lead questions should be formed with the maxim of six Ws that include what, why, when, where, which, and who. The supporting questions are constructed using interrogative clues like how, if, and though. Common guidelines for developing the questions for qualitative research can be listed as follows:

- Design only a few general questions to permit participants to share information with you.
- Construct questions that are neutral but exploratory.
- Use polite and ethical language to frame questions.
- Structure direct questions with all respected to sentiments respondents and legal fit of conversation.
- Design and write lead questions and supporting questions to the research topic.
- Do not use many closed-ended questions that restrict the expressions of respondents.

In qualitative research, the research questions differ greatly from a research topic during the conversation with respondents. Such situation emerges when the researcher intercepts the responses and frames new questions instantly. Many inquisitive researchers face such problem and collect enormous information but are unable to streamline the responses.

Consequently, a large data gets redundant and cannot be used in the analysis. The research topic is a broad area, in which a central phenomenon is woven around the key concept, idea, or process intended by the researcher to study through qualitative research (Creswell 2005). Once the research questions are drafted, the researcher should examine the questions to validate the response trend and the hidden attributes. Good research questions are researchable, clearly stated, theoretically motivated, and involve applied concepts to drive respondent to reveal his opinion (Bradley 2001). This process of evaluating the research questions consumes a considerable amount of time and effort.

Qualitative research requires both lead and supporting questions to acquire information comprehensively while conducting interviews. Lead questions trigger kick-off of interview process to obtain base information and set the scenario for further data collection. These questions should include direct questions six Ws comprising what, when, where, who, why, and how, and encourage response of subjects on the given situation. The researcher should give the respondents enough space to share their perceived experience during the information-gathering process. Sometimes respondents are sensitive to direct questions, so the lead questions should be structured based on framing questions indirectly seeking opinion on statements, referred reviews, indirect personal questions, and plans and motives. Researchers pursuing information through the qualitative sources should be trained in structuring direct, indirect, and incepting questions to obtain quality information from the respondents. Interceptive questions are derived from the continuing response with a view to gain in-depth information. Such questions do not have just one correct answer but might provoke parallel or counter questions to stimulate diverse or supplementary responses. Intercept surveys are conducted in-person, generally in a public place or business. For instance, interviewers might approach subjects leaving a restaurant and ask to interview them about their experiences. Interviewers ask the questions or simply explain the project and give the questionnaire to the respondent to fill out. The surveys might be completed on paper or any electronic device. Intercept interviews appear to be a great method for obtaining data for a research project. On-site interviews provide top-of-mind feedback of the respondents. However, it is necessary to develop the lead questions that could be responded with the evidential support. Such interpretive questions generate the most engaging discussions and might emerge with several different "correct answers."

A researcher must be truly interested and passionate about what is to be studied and should get involved in administering the questions to respondents. Such indulgence of investigator would help in scenario setting for administering questionnaire and information acquisition creating adequate interest among respondents. The thoroughness of researchers on the subject would fill a knowledge gap among respondents, drive respondents follow through the research process and reach staying close to the research goals (Farber 2006). However, research questions are not the same questions that are presented during the process of interviewing participants within the study. Research questions are the most important facets within the qualitative study and should be open-ended at large. A researcher must develop skills that allow gaining trust with the participant being interviewed so that responses that are not always positive will be given to provide a clearer picture and provide more details to the story of respondents. Qualitative research questions should be open-ended also to help investigator keep an open mind. These questions guide the research study, but at the same time allow subquestions and incepting questions to pave the way for new and emerging questions (Ohman 2005).

Developing good research ideas is both a science and an art. The researcher should develop knowledge on theoretical foundations and learn the ethical parameters on conducting qualitative research. Initially, as the research decides upon an approach to utilize in the research process, research directors and sponsors should encourage the researcher to develop research questions that would expand the knowledge on the topic of research and enhance the scope of information acquisition. In order to expand the research knowledge base, the research proposal should be meticulously reviewed and information to be acquired through the taxonomy of research questions (Bradley 2001).

The principal concern in developing a qualitative study is composing good research questions to ensure quality information. Most researchers, who are used to conduct quantitative research, feel uncomfortable working with the qualitative research as it is often challenging to compose research questions and conduct content analysis. Developing appropriate qualitative research questions can be practiced by drafting an exploratory research question, and then conducting a number of studies to clarify the research approach and define key terms. In this manner, more specific, narrow questions can evolve and provide a clear direction for the study (Frankel and Devers 2000). A qualitative researcher may even conduct a literature review of the initial research questions, or conduct a small study on the research questions, to determine whether the research questions are researchable. Accordingly, an appropriate scale can be developed by the researcher, or adapted based on the previous studies (Law 2004).

Digital Interactions

Social media communication is one of the most common and effective interventions in business communication, and in forming the interpersonal relationship. Young consumers are the next generation of loyal customers. Those with effective communication platforms tend to have higher opportunities to interact with peers and post them with their observations on marketplace and shopping dynamics. To disseminate their ideas among the peers, it is important to speak their language independently. Often the voice of customer with specific language skills may be difficult for the companies to match with their corporate communication patterns. The growth of technology-led social media communication channels has offered catalytic drive for electronic word-of-mouth communication since the beginning of the 21st century. More and more consumers use Web 2.0 tools such as online discussion forums, consumer review sites, weblogs, social network sites, and the like to communicate their opinions and exchange product information.

In addition, user-generated content in the form of online customer reviews has been found to significantly influence consumers' purchasing decisions. While word-of-mouth communication on the various Internet platforms has some characteristics in common with the traditional channel of communication, it is different from traditional ways of interpersonal communication in several dimensions. Information in traditional word-of-mouth is usually exchanged in private conversations or dialogues. It is therefore difficult to pass the information on to any individual who is not present when and where the information is exchanged.

The informal communication channel, which is largely dominated by the word-of-mouth content, may exhibit working within a framework of "who says what to whom and with what effect," social communication includes four major elements (Cheung et al. 2012):

- The *communicator* (*source*) refers to the person who transmits the communication.
- The *stimulus* (*content*) refers to the message transmitted by the communicator.
- The *receiver* (*audience*) is the individual who responds to the communication.
- The *response* (*main effect*) is made to the communicator by the receiver.

Existing interpersonal communication theories describe word-of-mouth behavior with a focus on face-to-face interaction, which illustrates that the communicators are in close proximity and can significantly influence the buying behavior of consumers in a marketplace (Knapp and Daly 2002). Informal communication theories based on the principles of social cognition and interpersonal relationship development from social psychology suggest that, given enough time to develop peer interactions, individuals can create fully formed impressions of others based solely on the verbal content on Internet portals. It is imperative that marketers understand how these impressions affect the assessment and the use of word-of-mouth information about products, brands, and firms, and consequential consumer behavior, both spatially and temporally, through the virtual platforms (Brown et al. 2007).

Large manufacturers of consumer goods recognize the added benefit of the Internet, especially the one-to-one relationships that it offers. Some large manufacturers have used the Internet to introduce customized shopping options, thus becoming retailers themselves and providing yet another challenge to the traditional store owner. It is observed that shoppers can choose the hair, eye and dress color of the doll they purchase by visiting the Barbie website of Mattel Company where shoppers may feel different, as they get service the traditional stores cannot offer. Consumers through Internet shopping gradually reveal their demographics and purchasing patterns, including date of birth, average spending, product preferences, and hobbies. Web-based businesses largely use this information as a platform to create an interactive loyalty program and database marketing. Although consumers can research high-price items such as cars and real estate via the Internet by analyzing the information on the attributes of offerings, the deal is still more effectively done face to face as confidence of buyers is boosted in personal negotiation. A retailer provides necessary personal contact the Internet cannot offer. However, in future, a successful retail store must build upon what the Internet cannot offer and add value to its customer's shopping experience by giving them that "something extra" to ensure continued patronage. In contrast, certain industries such as music industry have won a significant percentage of the market away from retail outlets. There will always be a place for retailers that serve impulsive and recreational purchasers, and for those who sell products that don't sell well over the Internet. The conventional retail stores need to reinvent store ambience as often their online competitors compete offline and online.

The social media backed by the Internet has changed the style of communication among consumer, companies, and the associated market players. Social media websites are designed to carry verbal and nonverbal communication with stimulus contents to attract millions of users, many of whom integrate the sites into their daily lives and business practices. Thus, social media allow users to connect with peers, companies, and brands irrespective of individual familiarity by adding them to networks of friends (Zhang and Daugherty 2009). Firms deploying marketing strategies through interactive and addressable communications within the social media platforms, improve their corporate image and products and services in various consumer communities. There are commonly six key elements that drive the interpersonal communications in the social media including love and passion, self-connection, interdependence, commitment, intimacy, and brand quality (Fournier 1998)

Consumer socialization among peers is driven with the dynamism of the social media, which encourages market-based interactions among the peers. Blogs, instant messaging, and social networking sites all provide communication tools that make the socialization process easy and convenient. Virtual communities easily socialize new incumbents into common and special interest groups and help them quickly learn task-related knowledge and skills through their interactions with other members. Besides quick inductions of members in the virtual groups, the inflow of consumers to social media websites is increasing and helping them communicate with others and find information to help them make various consumption-related decisions. The grapevine effect of the social media also facilitates education and information analysis among the members as the socialization agents within the informal groups provide vast product information and evaluations quickly (Taylor et al. 2011). Some studies reveal that peer communications influence consumers to such an extent that they convert others into virtual shoppers while some retailers also encourage social media communication by setting up tell-a-friend functions on websites.

The enormous growth of social media platforms and its usage among stakeholders has given marketers a compelling new avenue for conducting qualitative research. Many consumer products companies like Kellogg's (diet cereals brand), Mars Chocolate Companies (M&M brand), and Samsung (consumer electronics) have learnt and developed best practices from pilot researches leveraging Google Plus for consumer insights research. To test the viability of use of social media to conduct structured, qualitative consumer research, Google partnered with two research companies to run four pilot studies using Google Plus in October 2012. The research methods were woven around the videos and behavioral logs of social media users. Live Hangouts with participants were conducted with focus group discussions, while other social media users were engaged in specific activities like watching and evaluating advertisements on You-Tube together, or a group brainstorm using a third party Google Hang-out applications. The behavioral logs were analyzed using Google Docs. The smartphone owners were asked to log their wireless data usage over the course of a day via a pre-designed Google Docs form linked within an event.

Social institutions play significant role in nurturing the cultural heritage, which is reflected in the individual behavior. Such institutions including family, education, political structures, and the media, affect the ways in which people relate to one another, organize their activities to live in harmony with one another, teach acceptable behavior to succeeding generations, and govern themselves. The status of gender in society, the family, social classes, group behavior, age groups, and how societies define decency and civility, are interpreted differently within every culture. Social institutions are a system of regulatory norms and rules of governing actions in pursuit of immediate ends in terms of their conformity with the ultimate common value system of a community. They constitute underlying norms and values making up the common value system of a society. Institutions are intimately related to, and derived from, the value attitudes common to members of a community. This establishes institutions as primarily moral phenomena, which leads to enforce individual decisions on all human needs including economic and business-related issues. The primary means for enforcement of norms is the moral authority, whereby an individual obeys the norm because that individual believes that the norm is good for its own sake.

Social media, on one hand, spreads peer communication, while it prompts the marketing companies to stay responsive to the issues raised within the informal networks, on the other. Marketers can filter the social media communication and develop appropriate insights in the creation of useful concepts such as market and customer orientations, disseminate marketing knowledge, and strategies toward enhancing the customer value. Many organizations have successfully inculcated the practice of converging the social media information with development of marketing strategy. Although social network effects seem to have earned its place in business organizations, major differences remain in how organizations are market- or customer-oriented, how they *organize* and *operationalize* their marketing activities, and how they use marketing knowledge. Moreover, many marketing problems have not yet been solved through the social networks, for example, how to make organizations competitive, how to improve the capabilities of operational staff, and how to organize marketing activities to satisfy stakeholders' aims (operationalization). Marketing scientists may need to assist in the search for these answers by actively participating with the social networks and communication anchors.

Summary

Defining justifiable research problem is a challenging task for the qualitative researchers. The four major approaches to explore the defined problems through qualitative inquiry include explorative, experimental, casual, and action research in social laboratories. While describing the process of qualitative research nine important hybrid insights comprising identify, define, describe, inspire, explore, prioritize, analyze, draw inferences, and generalize have been discussed in this chapter, which supports various arguments on conducting qualitative research. Researchers choose one of the two common types of research designs, exploratory and experimental research design, which can fit into the qualitative research methodologies. Qualitative researchers also use nomothetic approach combining with observations during the in-depth interviews or participatory research appraisals to measure the personality related factors. The scope of qualitative research spans across cross-sectional studies that collect data from two or more sections of a sample based on the geo-demographic differences within the target community. In qualitative inquiries, the research designs are flexible and revised in view of the problem ecosystem, and attributes of the sample population for research in study area. Synthesis in qualitative inquiries are always debatable as they are intangible, being based on the opinions that cause subjectivity in drawing conclusions. Qualitative research questions are largely open-ended and provide ample space to the respondent to express. Content analysis has three distinct approaches comprising conventional, directed, or summative.

References

Agee, J. 2009. "Developing Qualitative Research Questions: A Reflective Process." *International Journal of Qualitative Studies in Education* 22, no. 4, pp. 431–47.

Bradley, D.B. 2001. "Developing Research Questions Through Grant Proposal Development." *Educational Gerontology* 27, no. 4, pp. 569–81.

Burck, C. 2005. "Comparing Qualitative Research Methodologies for Systemic Research: The Use of Grounded Theory, Discourse Analysis and Narrative Analysis." *Journal of Family Therapy* 27, no. 3, pp. 237–62.

Cash, P.J. 2018. "Developing Theory-driven Design Research." *Design Studies* 56, no. 1, pp. 84–119.

Casteleyn, J., A. Mottart, and K. Rutten. 2009. "How to Use Facebook in Your Market Research." *International Journal of Market Research* 51, no. 4, pp. 439–47.

Coghlan, D., and M. Brydon-Miller. 2014. *The Sage Encyclopedia of Action Research*. Thousand Oaks, CA: Sage.

Dev, C.S., and K.L. Keller. 2014. "Brand Revitalization." *Cornell Hospitality Quarterly* 55, no. 4, pp. 333–41.

Gibson, G., A. Timlin, S. Curran, and J. Wattis. 2004. "The Scope for Qualitative Methods in Research and Clinical Trials in Dementia." *Age and Ageing* 33, no. 4, pp. 422–26.

Hsieh, H.F., and S.E. Shannon. 2005. "Three Approaches to Qualitative Content Analysis." *Qualitative Health Research* 15, no. 9, pp. 1277–88.

Hyde, K.F. 2000. "Recognizing Deductive Processes in Qualitative Research." *Qualitative Market Research: An International Journal* 3, no. 2, pp. 82–90.

Isaacs, A.N. 2014. "An Overview of Qualitative Research Methodology for Public Health Researchers." *International Journal of Medicine and Public Health* 4, no. 4, pp. 318–23.

Kahneman, D., and A. Tversky. 1996. "On the Reality of Cognitive Illusions." *Psychological Review* 103, no. 3, pp. 582–91.

Knapp, M.S. 2017. "The Practice of Designing Qualitative Research on Educational Leadership: Notes for Emerging Scholars and Practitioner-Scholars." *Journal of Research on Leadership Education* 12, no. 1, pp. 26–50.

Koro-Ljungberg, M., and R. Bussing. 2013. "Methodological Modifications in a Longitudinal Qualitative Research Design." *Field Methods* 25, no. 4, pp. 423–40.

Lachal, J., A. Revah-Levy, M. Orri, and M.R. Moro. 2017. "Metasynthesis: An Original Method to Synthesize Qualitative Literature in Psychiatry." *Frontiers in Psychiatry* 8, p. 269.

Magids, S., A. Zorfas, and D. Leemon. 2015. *The New Science of Customer Emotions*. Boston, MA: Harvard Business School Publishing.

Markus, H.R., and S. Kitayama. 1991. "Culture and the Self: Implications for Cognition, Emotion, and Motivation." *Psychological Review* 98, no. 2, pp. 224–53.

Murphy, P. 2017. "Design Research: Aesthetic Epistemology and Explanatory Knowledge." *She Ji: The Journal of Design, Economics, and Innovation* 3, no. 2, pp. 117–32.

Noble, S.M., D.L. Haytko, and J. Phillips. 2009. "What Drives College-age Generation Y Consumers?" *Journal of Business Research* 62, no. 6, pp. 617–28.

Polit, D.F., and C.T. Beck. 2010. "Generalization in Quantitative and Qualitative Research: Myths and Strategies." *International Journal of Nursing Studies* 47, no. 11, pp. 1451–58.

Rajagopal, A. 2018. *Marketing Research: Fundamentals, Process, and Implications*. Hauppauge, New York, NY: Nova Publishers.

Seemann, J. 2012. "Where the Quantitative Meets, Qualitative." *Rotman Magazine*, Fall, pp. 57–61.

Stringer, E. 2007. *Action Research*. Los Angeles: Sage.

Szyjewska-Bagińska, J., and Z. Szyjewski. 2018. "Selected Problems of Contemporary Research on Behavior." *Procedia Computer Science* 126, pp. 1748–57.

Taguchi, N. 2018. "Description and Explanation of Pragmatic Development: Quantitative, Qualitative, and Mixed Methods Research." *System* 75, no. 1, pp. 23–32.

Thellefsen, T., B. Sørensen, and M. Danesi. 2013. "A Note on Cognitive Branding and the Value Profile." *Social Semiotics* 23, no. 4, pp. 561–69.

Trusov, M., A.V. Bodapati, and R.E. Bucklin. 2010. "Determining Influential Users in Internet Social Networks." *Journal of Marketing Research* 47, no. 4, pp. 643–58.

Usai, A., M. Pironti, M. Mital, and C.A. Mejri. 2018. "Knowledge Discovery Out of Text Data: A Systematic Review Via Text Mining." *Journal of Knowledge Management* 22, no. 7, pp. 1471–88

Wong, A.H., G.K. Tiyyagura, J.M. Dodington, B. Hawkins, D. Hersey, and M.A. Auerbach. 2017. "Facilitating Tough Conversations: Using an Innovative Simulation-Primed Qualitative Inquiry in Pediatric Research." *Academic Pediatrics* 17, no. 8, pp. 807–13.

CHAPTER 3

Information Management in Qualitative Research

Overview

There is always enormous amount of information in qualitative research due to liberal conversations in the field interviews during ethnographic and phenomenological studies. Hence, management of qualitative information is a major challenge among researchers. A database of qualitative information is usually unorganized and complex. Management of qualitative information essentially needs to be transformed into a system with the basic function of maintaining narrative information for its retrieval on demand to analyze the contents. This chapter discusses the fundamentals of qualitative data management and explains the care to be ensured for maintenance of the data. Analysis of qualitative information has been discussed in five major sections including information acquisition, metaphor analysis techniques, transcription and content management, data coding and content analysis, and computer aided qualitative date analysis. The perspectives on information acquisition have been discussed in reference to instrument development, information acquisition, and retrieval process. Data analysis process has been illustrated explaining how to synchronize the contents analysis categorical questions of the research instrument. In the consecutive discussion, this chapter also converses with the metaphor elicitation technique to analyze the information emerging out of conscious and subconscious mind on effects of imagery. Transcription techniques, data coding, and content analysis process with conventional wisdom and computer-aided qualitative data analysis systems have also been discussed in this chapter.

Principles of Qualitative Data Management

Managing qualitative information is complex as it is intangible. Information statements, phrases, quotes, observations, and storyboards are related to the point of expression timeline. Meanings of the information inputs change when reviewed on another period or if the same information is read repeatedly over time. The validity of information also changes as the time advances, unlike the numbers that reveal a firm view in quantitative research. However, qualitative research provides rich data on a specific phenomenon important to the thesis of the research, and may offer in-depth information for critical analytics to deliver the expected conclusion. Data management in qualitative research encompasses the elements of human cognition, expression, confidentiality, statements leading to evidences, and data ownership. Therefore, data storage, record keeping, and data sharing is a critical process in qualitative research that deserves researchers' attention. Qualitative research provides a profound representation of a phenomenon that is evidenced in the field research. The information on the phenomenon reveals the richness of a study. Data in qualitative research broadly include field notes, data recording, transcriptions, memos, and cognitive analytics. Data management in qualitative research is defined as a designed structure for systematizing, categorizing, and filing the materials to make them efficiently retrievable and duplicable (Lin 2009).

Management of qualitative data is often difficult due to various cognitive, social, and operational factors emerging during the study. Many times, researchers are not aware of the expected volume of information despite the sample population of subjects being specified. The data emerging out of qualitative inquiries are scattered as they are stored in scattered sources like audio-visual and field notes. Data stored in audiovisual devices need to be transcribed to be documented and stored in electronic files or in categorically arranged paper folders. In either case, transcription of data from audiovisual sources is always risk averse of "content-corruption." Physical loss of information documented on borrowed devices or theft of digital information from open networks or unprotected cloud-based domain causes major risk in qualitative research. Sometimes, file names create confusion in finding which interview transcript is the most complete one. However, the previous problems can be avoided if the qualitative information is arranged systematically in the coded arrays with a data tracking provision. If the researchers are not using any qualitative information analysis software such as QDA or NVivo, the data can be managed well in using Excel application, where data can be stored using appropriate codes. This arrangement would facilitate categorical data retrieval for making interpretations and drawing inferences. Proper data management allows researchers to accumulate information in various forms or locations by maintaining the security of the data for meta-analysis and data interpretations in the longitudinal studies.

Qualitative information can be organized by drawing a roadmap indicating the area, subjects, taxonomy of questions, observations, and social concerns. By developing a roadmap, organized qualitative data allow researchers to analyze specific research questions. Researchers can use a reflective process of managing the data generated in qualitative research to better systematize their data (Halcomb and Davidson 2006). Qualitative data management includes various concerns, not limited to confidentiality, protection of subjects of sample population covered in the study, and problems of data storage, sharing, and ownership. Confidentiality is one of the major responsibilities of a researcher, and a professional commitment to the participants in the qualitative inquiry process (Pinch 2000). One of the principal commitments of researchers conducting qualitative inquiries is to protect the information of participants in all possible ways. Building cohesive rapport with the participants is also important condition for the researchers because it promotes nonhierarchical relationship between the researcher and the subject. Researchers must show the participants that the researcher will treat their data with respect and maintain privacy. Ethnographic techniques would ensure confidentiality by evaluating the privacy, like anonymity of all interlinked elements of subjects in case of high-risk studies (Woogara 2015).

Reflective diaries maintained by qualitative researchers help in preventing them from committing the same mistakes during the research process. Unless prevented by the subjects of investigation, it is advised to share the research data in many ways to advance knowledge in sociocultural, ethnic, cognitive, and health care fields. Many journals publishing research studies advocate researchers to store the data on cloud-based domains and deliver the details of digital object identifier (DOI). Data ownership needs to be defined, and accountability of investigators should be fixed accordingly. In many instances, data might be owned by the research funders, research institutions, research participants (in some cases), or investigators. In qualitative research, research participants are often highly involved with the data collected, which may make them feel authoritative on the information (Manderson, Kelaher, and Woelz-Stirling 2001).

Community partnerships with qualitative researchers has a sensitive line involved in collaborative, qualitative research projects on social and preventive health such as incidence and control of HIV infection and other communicable diseases. Research on the project generates substantial data with the potential to impact health policy. These data often include highly confidential and sensitive narratives, requiring strict data management practices to protect the data from damages during sharing and information analysis. Often, such high-risk qualitative research projects go beyond the structured instrument during the in-depth and open-ended interviews. Therefore, during the process of information analysis, inclusion of unprotected narratives might deeply affect the personal life and cause grief, hardship, and inconsistency among the subjects. Therefore, researchers must develop a process to communicate the results on selected variables that would protect the anonymity and sensitivity of subjects' information. This process would require a balance between information acquisition and reporting important findings of the study (Hardy et al. 2016).

Qualitative Information Analysis

Analysis of qualitative information is an art and science. Acquiring information through qualitative instruments, analyzing contents, and drawing inferences is a scientific approach, while blending such inferences with informal observations, field notes, and public views is an art in qualitative research, as it needs a rationale and community sensitive vision. Qualitative data analysis holds the major tasks of classification of data, analysis of information by variable segments, and interpretation of the results. Developing statements about implicit and explicit conclusions by carrying out the structural analysis of meanings embedded in the information provide inadequate support to interpret the qualitative information. In this process interpretations of subjective and social meanings are often complex. Qualitative data analysis should be aimed at discovering and describing issues in the study area, social and family structures, and decision processes among the stakeholders in society, family, and business. Unlike statistical analysis of quantitative data, qualitative data analysis should be divided into two phases: initial and final. In some high-risk studies like technology diffusion, new products development, security risks, health care studies, medicinal trials, and sensitive social topics of research, an intermediate phase is also created to control the analysis and reporting anomalies. The initial phase of information analytics includes of a rough analysis of the material overviews, condensation, summaries. These tasks are followed by the final phase of a detailed analysis concerning elaboration of categories, hermeneutic interpretations, or predetermined identified social structures. Hermeneutics is the theory and methodology of interpretation developed for the interpretation of linguistically complex information such as biblical texts and philosophical texts. Such methodology might not be commonly required to analyze the consumer and business data unless it has some obscure script or linguistic parameters.

Most of the qualitative research projects like studying consumer behavior, corporate culture, and stakeholder values on business policies are able to derive specific or fragmented conclusions within consumer categories, clusters, or over temporal and spatial dimensions of the research. Such fragmented conclusions cause narrow scope of qualitative data in reference to its analytical implications. However, longitudinal qualitative studies conducted over temporal and spatial dimensions aim to arrive at generalizable statements by comparing wide-focused responses, cross-sectional information, and analyzing the strategic business or governmental documents. The analysis of qualitative data should encompass the following focuses to deliver the conclusions that can be generalized:

1. Describing a phenomenon
2. Comparing information across subjects, space, and time
3. Explanations to lead and peripheral analysis, and
4. Developing an inductive theory

A systematically organized information within the psychosocial and developmental arrays across spatial and temporal dimensions help researchers in describing a phenomenon and comparing the evolution of related factors across subjects and geo-demographic segments. Chronological information offers researchers relevant indicators to explain thematically the qualitative research thesis and lead peripheral analysis. Accordingly, inductive theory concerning the research can be established. In carrying out the analysis of qualitative information, the subjective experiences such as observations of the researcher play a significant contribution. Another factor that intervenes in the analytical process include a social situation, which needs to be explained in reference to its consequences on the family and public life of the subjects. Social practices and routines also offer relevant hints to explain the background of the social analytical procedures using the qualitative information. The theoretical roots of this approach outgrows from ethnomethodology, which is one of the principal approaches to collect qualitative data.

Over the years, the focus of information analysis has turned toward interpreting the phenomena through narratives and ethnographic descriptions. The trend of reporting qualitative studies has turned more systematic and conventional in the context of writing essays, coding, and data arraying with the help of software programs and packages for computer aided data analysis (Banner and Albarran 2009). During the mid-1980s, the qualitative information analysis led to development of static and dynamic social paradigms based on the interactivity of key indicators of a research study. In this context, the evaluation of research and findings became central to methodological discussions. In the following period, the interpretation of narratives and storyboards have replaced paradigm analytics and deductive theories. The pattern of analysis of qualitative information gradually shifted to grand narratives and inductive theories explaining the local, historical situations, and socially felt problems. Accordingly, the data analysis adapted to experimental writing, linking issues of qualitative research to public policies.

Acquiring Information

Qualitative methods include structured verbal interviews and free associations techniques (Danes et al. 2010) that can be used toward assessing consumer perceptions on behavioral branding. These methods improve the data collection process derived from more traditional scale-based approaches (Arora and Stoner 2009).While sharing experience on the structured research instrument, subjects experience cognitive, rational, emotional, social, and cultural attributes while dealing with brands. In the case of consumers, such data collection approaches allow researchers to map perceptions of consumers on product, services, and brands anthropomorphically through personal interactions (Hooper 2011). Therefore, data can be effectively collected using semistructured verbal interviews. However, informal associations with the respondents help in supplementing the data through categorical observations. Acquiring qualitative information depends on the type of questions structured in the research instrument and the method of data collection opted during the study. Collecting information through the in-depth interviews provides ample scope of pooling comprehensive data for conducting multilayered content analysis. For collecting comprehensive and quality information through the in-depth interviews, following points need to be reviewed while preparing questions:

1. Design a few general questions to permit participants to share introductory information.
2. Construct questions that are neutral and nonjudgmental, but have the potential to explore comprehensive information during the interview process.
3. Use nonauthoritative, polite, and ethical language to structure the questions.
4. Structure direct questions with all respect to sentiments of the respondents and legal fit of conversation.
5. Design and list lead and supporting questions that are thematic to the research and match with the ecosystem of the study, and
6. Closed-ended questions are discouraged in the qualitative research instrument as they restrict the expressions of subjects and obstruct the rationale in thinking process.

In qualitative research, research questions differ greatly from the research topic during conversations with respondents. Such a situation emerges when the researcher intercepts the responses and frames new questions instantly. Most inquisitive researchers face such problem, they collect enormous information but are unable to streamline the responses. Consequently, a large data gets redundant, which cannot be used in the analysis. Research topic is a broad area, in which a central phenomenon is woven around the key concept, idea, or process intended to be studied by the researcher through qualitative research (Creswell 2005). Once research questions are drafted, the researcher should examine the questions to validate the response trend and the hidden attributes. Good research questions are researchable, clearly stated, theoretically motivated, and involve applied concepts to drive respondent to reveal their opinion (Bradley 2001). However, evaluating the research questions consumes a considerable amount of time and effort.

Qualitative research requires both lead and supporting questions to comprehensively acquire information while conducting interviews. The lead questions trigger kick-off of the interview process to obtain base information and set the scenario for further data collection. These questions should include direct questions (6W's) comprising what, when, where, who, why, and which, and encourage response of subjects on the given situation. A researcher should give the respondents enough space to share their perceived experience during the information gathering process. Sometimes respondents are sensitive to direct questions, so the lead questions should be framed indirectly seeking opinion on statements, referred reviews, indirect personal questions, and plans and motives. Researchers pursuing information through qualitative sources should be trained in structuring direct, indirect, and interceptive questions to obtain quality information from the respondents. Interceptive questions are derived from the continuing response with a view to gain in-depth information. Such questions do not have just one correct answer, they might provoke parallel or counter questions to stimulate diverse or supplementary responses. Intercept surveys are conducted in-person, generally in a public place or business. For instance, interviewers might approach the subjects leaving a restaurant and ask to interview them about their experiences. Interviewers ask questions or simply explain the project and give questionnaire to the respondent to fill out. The surveys might be completed on paper or any electronic device. Intercept interviews appear to be a great method for obtaining data for a research project. On-site interviews provide top-of-mind feedback of the respondents. However, it is necessary to develop the lead questions that could be responded with the evidential support. Such interpretive questions generate the most engaging discussions and might emerge with several different correct answers (Rajagopal 2018).

In order to explore comprehensive information from the subjects, the researcher must locate the key and community informants. Key informants are the subjects who have knowledge on the research theme and experience to respond to the questions, possess leadership quality, and have social or family responsibilities. Community informants are the local subjects who also share conversations on variety of questions during the fieldwork at the respective localities. If the researcher succeeds in building good relationships with the subjects, they develop confidence in sharing knowledge on the research topic and may become effective key informants. Key informants are not only useful for soliciting a lot of information on the research topic, but are also essential in locating other informants through their connection with, and knowledge of (sections of), the community. Unless researchers have experience with qualitative methodologies, interviewers should be trained in data collection and data transcription processes. Interviewers should learn role-playing, and watching or listening to the interview tapes scientifically. It is necessary to develop a que-sheet of information stored in tapes, which needs to be analyzed. The que-sheet should contain the core information, arguments, evidences, and creative ideas in reference to the concerned questions.

During the information collection process, skilled researchers show a genuine interest in interviewees and their responses. During the process of conducting in-depth interviews, researchers should be able to manage their social image and personality, and exhibit nonjudgmental attitude. It is common that most subjects use slangs in their responses. Therefore, the recorded interviews should be carefully listened, and appropriate meaning of slangs should to be derived. Researchers also need to develop the ability to observe verbal and nonverbal cues in the information to substantiate the contents of the subjects. The information acquisition process can be controlled by developing the following norms and standards:

- Ability to follow up responses with a view to explore emerging issues while adhering to the research instrument.
- Adopt "bridge and breach" techniques for information acquisition.

- Interrupt to move to next question / theme.
- Make connections / recognize contradictions.
- Use nondirective and noncommanding probes.

Researchers must pay attention to explore contemporary information from the subjects during the interview process. In this process, they may pose many peripheral and intercept questions, but must adhere to the broad perspective of the research instrument. It has been observed that subjects often need some logical support to build their responses due to temporary loss of context or memory per se. Researchers should possess the knowledge and skills to bridge such information gaps, and the skills to moderate the discussions and streamline the information flow, interrupt, or move to the next question breaching the time on the current question. However, researchers must stay nonjudgmental, noncommanding, and nondirective while conducting the interviews. The interviews can be moderated by guiding and explaining critical points of information. The quality of information is affected by the current state of mind of the subjects. Therefore, the *active* and *passive* subjects need to be managed by the researchers in reference to psychosocial cognition factors, beliefs, ethnicity, and emotions. Simultaneously, the discussions during the interview process need to be streamlined intermittently to ensure quality of information and eliminate on-field data redundancy. Before moving to the next question in the interview process, or concluding a section of information, researchers must summarize salient discussion points, and seek the endorsement by the subjects on the conclusion. However, while documenting or recording the information, small cues on the points of interest raised by the subjects need to be categorically noted. These cues would help the researchers explore further information on the emerging concerns of the subjects either by organizing additional interviews or through the text-data-mining approach. In the process of interviewing the subjects, unpleasant or irrelevant memories often shadow the principal point of discussion. Such memory inhibition must be filtered to avoid biases in information. Similarly, cognitive inhibition, which emerges due to mind's ability to surface irrelevance while discussing the uninterested or avoidable concerns, also needs to be controlled.

Information Retrieval and Learning Process

Researchers must develop skills to retrieve the memorized information and the information collected on the various devises. Despite enhanced interest in the mechanics of qualitative information retrieval in recent years, the extended qualitative data storage-retrieval and data reduction-analysis have been applied in some research studies. Common procedures for these tasks are not systematically examined or codified in the qualitative research. The five principles to be followed to ensure safe retrieval of the data include formatting, cross-referral, indexing including thesauri (lexica or vocabulary) design and cross-referencing, abstracting, and pagination (Levine 1985). The field work data is typically recorded in a sequence of the questions in the research instruments. The data related to the social interaction of the investigator and informant are documented in the field diary rather than linearly pointing to the topics under investigation.

The general models of data storage and retrieval for the field-based qualitative investigation are similar to the information management in library science. There are problems associated with qualitative databases, which need careful investigation specific to the nature of information that requires data storage and retrieval. Abstracting, index systems, thesaurus, storing descriptive data in digital file, and semantic textual analysis are some mechanical ways of developing information inventory that could help the researchers. Depending on the plans of the text analysis, new information can be generated by using codes, code definitions, code relationships, code–text relationships, hypertext linkages, and conceptual maps (MacQueen and Milstein 1999).

In the information retrieval process, researchers need to manage texts and phrases in retrieving the information besides the mechanical approaches to store and retrieve the data. Subjects often exhibit physical gestures and expressions to convey their views. Such incidences might happen with the subjects who are children, less educated, at high risk referring to health disorders, under civil protection, or facing terminal disease. Therefore, subjects need to be stimulated appropriately to retrieve memories and convey the right information during the study process. The memory retrieval process can be stimulated using the closed- and open-loop approaches. Closed-loop approach consists of sensory feedback or stimuli to cognitive dynamics and explores memory traces of subjects over space and time. Breaking the closed cognitive loop of subjects helps the researchers carry out perceptual mapping and interpretation. Open-loop approach helps the subjects pull out abstract memory and recall information with peripheral feedback or stimuli. Open-loop stimuli drive emotions and excitement among subjects during the interview process. Thus, researchers might observe rapid and aggressive physical movements, articulation, and novel expressions of subjects during personal interviews. Researchers must understand the cognitive ecosystem of the subjects, and manage the information emerging from conscious mind and stored in the subconscious memories. The coordination between self-congruence and referrals, perceptual mapping (spatial and temporal), connectivity between cognition, thoughts, and expressions must be clearly documented by the researchers during the information acquisition process.

Analyzing Data Through Research Instrument

A comprehensive research instrument used to collect information serves as an asset for carrying out sequential analytics of interconnected variables. Most research instruments are built around the statements such as "effective public policies improve the quality of social life." The validation of such statements by quantification and purposive interpretations would help in analyzing such qualitative statements. Other types of questions, as discussed in the following, need to be categorically analyzed:

- Descriptive questions
  - Limitations
  - Contents
  - Ethics
- Intercept questions
- Reverse questions
  - Respondent generated
  - Synthesized questions
- Funnel questions
- Pictorial questions

Descriptive questions form the core of a qualitative research instrument and widely influence the information analysis process. However, due to the comprehensive information embedded in descriptive responses, the limitation of the information in reference to the selected parameters like time, area, cost, economic benefits, social development, and quality of life should be fixed for analysis. Information analysis can be carried out on a case-by-case basis by arranging the responses in a consecutive order. The content analysis of descriptive information needs to be done moving from macro to micro perspectives. Intercept questions in the interview process are asked to comprehend the contextual information on the responses to the principal questions. Analysis of the peripheral information generated through the intercept questions (asked by the researcher and reverse questions (posed by the subject to the investigator) need to be categorically arranged and reviewed in reference to the core information collected during the study. Information generated through these questions provides a base for raising social arguments at the grassroots. Most researchers exhibit their enthusiasm in qualitative research by enchaining subjects into a series of thematic perspectives. However, researchers should take a categorical approach on drawing inferences and structuring arguments to synthesize such funneled information on random perspectives. Information analysis can be carried out in different tiers based on the taxonomy of questions in the research instrument. The systematic approach of information analysis leading to meta-analysis and meta-synthesis is shown in Figure 3.1.

Research questions can be broadly classified into three categories: conceptual, problem based, and knowledge-driven perspectives as shown in Figure 3.1. Tier-I analysis in qualitative research is suggested to explore the conceptual values of the subjects toward social and public ideas, surfacing radical thinking, and critically examining the public policies. The information analysis at Tier-II provides filtering of creative ideas, arguments, and descriptive contents on relational and contextual data. Researchers can compare the strengths and weaknesses of the information at this tier of analysis. The problem-based information contains responses based on the experience, facts, and critical understanding of problems. Such information should be analyzed on the background of needs, emotions, beliefs, trust, and expectation of the subjects. Accordingly, researchers can draw

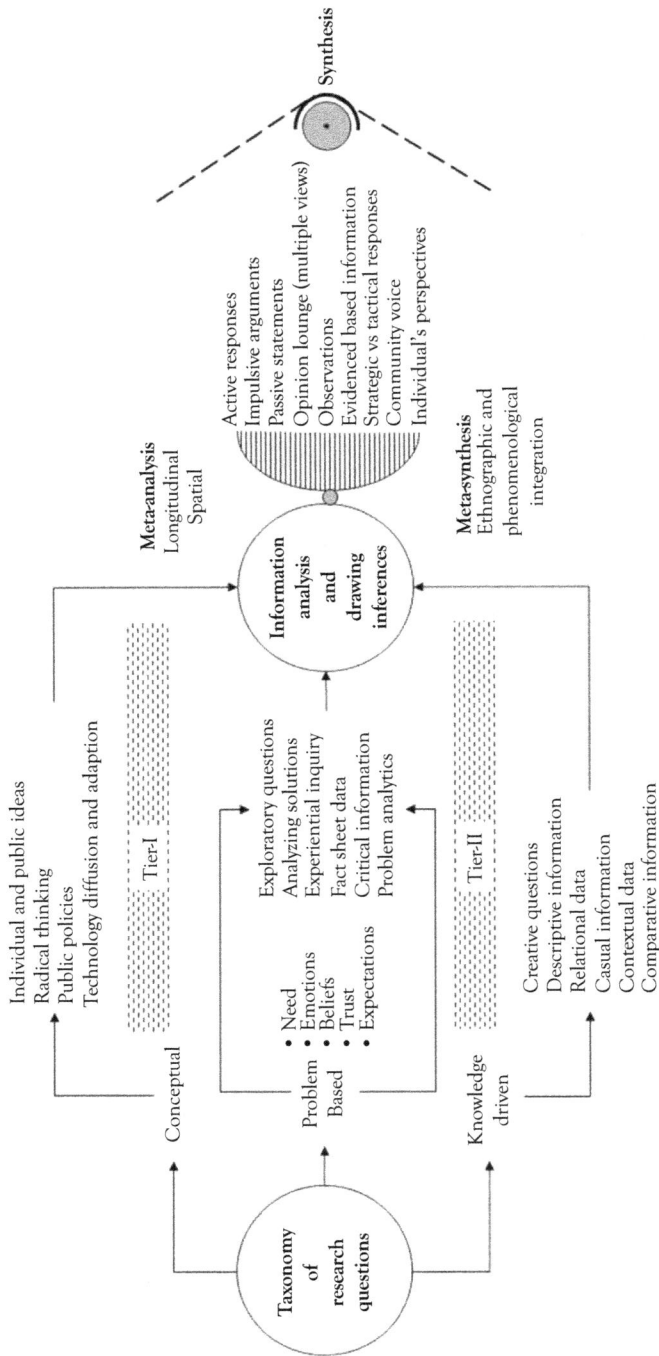

Figure 3.1 Systematic view of qualitative information analysis

inferences on active responses, impulsive arguments and evidence-based information. An opinion lounge can be set on an appropriate software like QDA, NVivo, or Excel, where a research can accommodate opinions of all the subjects and filter them according to their pragmatism and significance. Sometimes, the passive statements posed by the subjects also make a base for raising strong arguments in the qualitative research. Accordingly, the analysis across spatial and temporal dimensions can be planned as meta-analysis on the selected variables of the study. However, ethnographic and phenomenological studies could develop meta-synthesis by linking the vital arguments emerging out of the study.

Metaphor Elicitation Analysis

Qualitative researchers often face the metaphoric expressions of subjects while responding to the interview questions. A metaphor is an expression of speech that describes an object or action in an unrealistic way, but helps to explain an idea or draw a comparison. Broadly, in qualitative market research, a metaphor involves understanding and experiencing one product or service in terms of another. It elucidates the perception of the consumer on one product or service, as if it was different from its real image. Metaphors are central to understanding the human cognition as they invoke and express nonverbal imagery. Linguistic metaphors widely reflect underlying conceptualizations of experience in long-term memory. The nonverbal communications are considered as major touch points, in which researchers observe the neurophysical dynamics of the subjects.

Zaltman Metaphor Elicitation Technique (ZMET) is a milestone in measuring the cognitive moves of people on personality development perspectives. ZMET explores both conscious and unconscious thoughts, in order to understand people from inside at the deepest level possible. Ethnographers, who are involved in mapping the subconscious thoughts of their subjects, use this technique extensively. Qualitative researchers observe, and interact with, people in their most emotionally relevant environments, and combine metaphor elicitation methodology for deeper, more nuanced understanding of the perceptions of the subjects. In the ZMET analysis, researchers determines how effectively people's unconscious emotional drivers identify the meaning people co-create on the social or personal development standpoints. In this methodology, subjects collect a handful of images representing their thoughts and feelings about a particular topic, and each participant is interviewed using their images as a jumping-off point for discussion. This method is similar to participatory (rural) appraisals, in which subjects map their resources, identify problems, and suggest solutions.

The ZMET methodology involves the following key elements for cognitive analysis of information:

- Contextual stimuli
- Sensory cognition
- Episodic memory
- Rationale, metaphor, and anthropomorphism
- Emotional consequences
- Physio-psychological response
- Consumer traits and values
- Storytelling and storyboard analysis
- Verbal and nonverbal communication
- Controlled gestures, voice analytics, and neuro-imagery analysis

Contextual stimulus is a situation-based motivation given to the subject during the interview process in qualitative research. The situations are assessed in reference to behavioral status and the expected consequence of the stimulus on the subject. Therefore, opinions of the subjects on pictures vary widely and affect the real-time responses. For instance, a picture of a person who is looking at a food store might stimulate the subject contextually to reveal whether he had passed through such money crunch situation. The consequence of such contextual stimuli may be positive or depressing, which might affect the real-time response of the subject. Hence, researchers should understand the behavior of the subject before introducing any contextual stimuli.

Sensory cognition is a process, which moves from senses to the brain, to carry out cognitive analysis. The upstream sectors of synaptic hierarchy in the brain develop unimodal association with the features of sensation such as color, motion, form, and pitch, and encode them for cognitive analytics. However, complex sensory experiences such as objects, faces, word-forms, spatial locations, and sound sequences are encoded within downstream sectors of unimodal areas. Hence, colors and physical objects do drive the sensory cognition of subjects during the qualitative inquiry process. Inflexible bonds between sensation and action lead to instinctual and automatic behaviors that are often resistant to change, even when faced by negative consequences (Mesulam 1998). Such sensory cognition helps researchers explore the experiences-led responses over space and time.

Episodic memory is defined as the ability to cognitively recall and re-experience specific episodes from the personal past. It is an autobiographical memory mapping process, which is opposite to semantic memory that includes memory for generic, context-free knowledge. In the qualitative research, episodic memories can be documented as storytelling and the researchers can develop a storyboard for each subject. Episodic memories are consciously recollected memories related to personally experienced events, while the episodic remembrance is a dynamic process that draws upon mnemonic and non-mnemonic cognitive abilities. The retrieval of episodic memories is a useful tool to cognitively reconstruct past experiences following appropriate retrieval cues. Therefore, researchers should prompt episodic memories of the subjects and document them in the order of relevance (Wheeler and Ploran 2009).

The rationale of stimuli and appropriateness of metaphor reflect in building anthropomorphism among the subjects, which makes them impersonate an entity. Anthropomorphic expressions raise emotional and physio-psychological responses among the subjects. Such situations need to be handled carefully by the researchers, and should be recorded digitally if possible, which would be helpful to the researchers while analyzing the episodic memories. ZMET is widely used in the consumer research, and the social and developmental research. It helps in exploring the consumer traits and values through storytelling and storyboard analysis. This technique is based on verbal and nonverbal communication. However, active researchers also map the gestures, conduct voice analytics, and perform neuro-imagery analysis of the qualitative research studies.

Other analytical approaches that support ZMET include mind-mapping, semantic perceptions, and analyzing contents of metaphorical conversation. Mind mapping techniques were developed in the late 1960s, but only after the emergence of information and communication technologies, mind maps are being successfully applied in consumer behavior analysis, innovation management, and organizational behavior areas. Mind mapping can be done using software or can be drawn on a paper during the qualitative interview produces. This technique is useful to explore learning experiences that facilitate cognitive reflection, knowledge building, problem solving, inquiry, and critical thinking among the subjects. Using mind maps as an active learning strategy is an innovative technique used to facilitate exploring new ideas, developmental concepts, and experience-based elucidations. In the qualitative research, subjects can illustrate a vision, exhibit their contextual knowledge and creativity, and make associations about a central theme during this activity (Rosciano 2015). Semantics comprising contextual meanings, interrelated logics, and ideas can be documented during the qualitative research process as an outgrowth of mind mapping exercise. The lexical semantics can be plotted around the core idea and interlinked in reference to word meaning and symbiotic rationale.

Transcription and Content Management

The most challenging task in qualitative research is the transcription of information stored in electronic devices. Since the responses of subjects in qualitative research are lengthy and complex, interviews are often recorded in electronic devices and later transcribed to the text form. Transcribing appears to be a straightforward technical task, but in fact involves judgments of the researcher while protecting the contents of original data and its interpretation, omitting nonverbal dimensions of the interaction. The quality of transcribed data is often questionable due to convenience of data interpretation and less rigor in conserving the originality of the information. Often, the slang communication used in the responses cannot be transcribed verbatim, which causes bias in the information. It is also observed in various interviews that the responses of the subjects to various questions stay unclear, making it difficult for the researchers to transcribe under assumptions. For example, respondents might not be clear in responding to some questions about their family and health such as personal relations, family sickness, etc.

Transcription is necessary for open-ended responses, information of focus groups, observation, and individual interviews. Transcripts strengthen the data audit as researchers can review the text while listening to the interview recording. Qualitative inquiries can also be set up through digital networks. The interviews scheduled via Zoom conference have online transcription option, which allows the researcher to watch the recording and read the transcript simultaneously. All transcriptions should have the subject identifier tags to keep the anonymity of information. Transcription of language-specific conversations should be done contextually instead of verbatim transcription. While transcribing the information, researchers may also be benefitted by field notes, flow charts, and figures drawn during the field study. Researchers should also learn about various transcription approaches as discussed as follows:

- Videos interviews
- Audio recordings
- Transcription and translation
- Partial or selective transcripts
- Sign language transcription
- Inference based transcription- Managing qualitative interviews with children and physically challenging people

Video interviews can be automatically transcribed using some software as discussed in the pretext. However, audio recordings need to be carefully transcribed by the researchers without altering the meaning of narration. Verbatim translations often damage the meaning of narrations. Hence, translations should be done in contextual sense without affecting the contents of narrations. Partial transcription refers to transcribing narrations along with interpretation of nonverbal information like charts, images, and semantic notes. Certified interpreters must carry out sign language transcription, though there are automatic sign language translation software like Sign All. The researcher may also opt for inference-based transcription for managing qualitative interviews with children and physically challenging people.

Visual data are more difficult to process since they take a huge length of time to transcribe, and there are fewer conventions to represent visual elements on a transcript. The meanings of utterances are profoundly shaped in the way something has been said. Transcriptions need to be very detailed to capture features of talk such as emphasis, speed, tone of voice, timing and pauses, as these elements can be crucial for interpreting data. Transcription involves close observation of data through repeated careful listening (and/or watching), and this is an important first step in data analysis. This familiarity with data, and attention to what is actually there rather than what is expected, can facilitate realizations or ideas, which emerge during analysis (Pope 2000).

Transcribing the spoken language and slang expressions emerging out of an interview or a focus group is yet another challenge for the researcher as the text needs modification of transcription rules. The interview transcription generally results in about 20 percent loss in content and needs focus on slangs, regional language, and peripheral information. Usually the content of the language is of main interest, but there are possibilities to enrich the text with additional aspects. A transcription system contains a set of exact rules on how spoken language is transformed into written text. Therefore, researchers must complete the pretranscription tasks as listed as follows:

- Familiarization with the instrument
- Recalling data collection scenario
- Referring to researcher's journal/ agenda
- Key indicators of data collection
- Analyzing behavior of respondents
- Decide pattern:
- Verbatim transcription
- Selective transcription
- Comprehensive transcription

Before starting the transcription, researchers should reorient themselves with the research instrument, familiarize with the questions, and recall the interview scenario, so that contextual inferences can be developed. Referring to researcher's journal (diary) would help in supplementing the transcribed contents of narrations. There are different transcription protocols that need to be followed during the qualitative research process:

- Selective protocol: In this process, the researcher selectively transcribes the audio recording of the interview, which is relevant for the research question. Interviews often contain extensive introductory parts, auxiliary discussions, motivational standpoints, and explanation of the research question that constitute the contents and quality of information and compliance of the interviewee. However, selection of contents made by the researchers is sometimes biased, and it adversely influences the transcription process and text interpretation. If the interviews are long and narrative in nature, the selection of narration for transcription is a difficult task. Researcher should make a que-sheet of narration and match it with the required response to questions and research propositions.

- Comprehensive protocol: A researcher may like to transcribe the complete contents of recorded interviews of respondents without selecting the sections in parts if the information is neither ambiguous nor too open to interpretations. However, if a researcher is interested in transcribing only the contents, a comprehensive protocol might be sufficient. The researcher or his transcribing team reads or listens the language, pauses at regular intervals to synchronize narration with the text, and sums up the main contents. Use of an automatic speech recognition program could be useful for the transcription provided the narration is compatible to the software program.

- Verbatim transcription: This is an unusual practice and should be avoided as the etymology and contextual narrations differ by language. A word might have different meaning while transcribing into another language. For example, "Nova" might refer to a brand in Mexico and indicate the verbatim meaning as "doesn't go." The verbatim transcription is done word for word for citing the opinions of interviewees or preparing quotes, but all utterances like hmm or aha, and decorating words like, right, you know, and yeah are discarded. The researcher produces a coherent text simple to understand but representing the original wording and grammatical structure during the transcription. Short-cut articulation and dialect are translated into standard language, for example, c'mon indicates "come on." However, in this process, dialect formulations, fillers, and articulation are maintained as in the narration.

Verbatim transcription of qualitative information has become a common data management strategy in association with the technology applications. It is being actively used in public health and nursing research, and has been proved effective to the analysis and interpretation of verbal data. The benefits of verbal data are becoming more widely popular in social marketing, consumer research, and health care studies, and interviews are being increasingly used to collect information for a wide range of qualitative research studies. In addition to purely qualitative investigations, there has been significant increase in opinion-led research studies. It is important to set-up the contextual rules for transcription. It is necessary to define a system of transcription specific to region and language. Deciding which one of these systems to use depends on the research question, the characteristics of the language, and the theoretical background of the analysis. However, one of the major challenges in transcription of information arises when the narration is supported with nonverbal illustrations like pictures and charts. Successful transcription could be done by following the transcription process as discussed in the following:

- Intermittent listening/viewing
- Developing que-sheet
- Sentence-by-sentence transcription
- Reconfirmation of transcript with original response
- Approvals of respondents
- Cross-references to questions
- Editing transcripts
- Highlighting contents/ indexing /cataloguing

In order to ensure successful transcription of narrations from the audiovisual devises, it is necessary to listen intermittently, develop a que-sheet of significant points, and set the sequencing of transcription. If the narrations are small, sentence-by-sentence transcription can be done.

However, all transcriptions need to be revalidated from the original narration or the subjects, if available. Sometimes the subjects repeat the same responses for the contextually relevant questions. Such repetitions might create biases in interpreting the responses. Hence, transcripts also need to be edited rationally by highlighting significant contents and developing an index of keywords. This process would help researchers in eliminating the outliers from the data. Outliers are inconsistent in providing information and do not validate the data throughout the study. Such data must be removed from coding and content analysis.

Transcription in qualitative research constitutes a principal segment of the data analysis process, which should be clearly disclosed in the study design of a project. It is therefore essential for a transcription method to be congruent with the theoretical maxims of a specific investigation should be used. This practice determines the potential to use alternate processes for managing verbal interview data over the conventional verbatim transcription techniques if they are consistent with the underlying philosophy of the study design.

Data Coding and Content Analysis

Data coding in qualitative research is a field-information identification tag, which facilitates researchers to carry out systematic information analysis. A code in qualitative inquiry is most often a set of alphanumeric fields or short phrases that symbolically assign the study area, subject's identity such as age, gender, social hierarchy occupation and so on. and order of interview, language, data, time, and other significant identification marks. It is a summative, salient, essence-capturing, and/or evocative attribute for a narrative or visual data. Such code can be easily segmented for arraying the interview transcripts, participant observation, field notes, journals, documents, literature, artifacts, photographs, video, websites, and e-mail correspondence. In developing a storyboard of the interviews, the portion of data to be coded during first cycle coding process can range in magnitude from a single word to longer phrase to a stream of moving information. In second cycle coding processes, the coded portions can be the exact same units, longer passages of text, and even a reconfiguration of the codes themselves developed thus far. Such coding exercise can be

Table 3.1 **Coding example for narratives in qualitative research**

Subject Tag	Narrative	Content Analysis Code
S1-NY-Brand-M-32-En-Ex-100318-113025	...when I use vogue brands, I feel confident, and it allows me to enter high profile social circles...	Trend-personality Sub Contents Code: Anthropomorphic behavior (AB)
S2-NJ-Brand-F-24-En-St-100318-113025	...vogue in the market is created by social interaction and behavioral brands are positioned by word-of-mouth	Trend-co-creation Sub Contents Code: Innovation and consumer value (ICV)

done for longitudinal qualitative studies, which are spread across the geo-demographic and temporal indicators. For example, coding of narratives in the qualitative research can be used as discussed in Table 3.1.

It can be seen from the Table 3.1 that subject tag can hold the information like subject identity (S-1), study area (NY), construct classification (Brand), gender (M), age (32), language (En-English), occupation (Ex-executive), and date and time of the interview. The relevant narrative can be cited in the adjacent column, and content analysis code can be generated. Such coding would facilitate researchers to carry out contents analysis systematically. The content analysis code can be further subcoded to indicate the section of analysis in which the information can be used as a subsequent effect. In Table 3.1, the subcontents analysis codes refer to personality leading to anthropomorphic behavior (AB), and co-creation of trends leads to innovation and consumer value (ICV). However, while developing subcodes for contents analysis, researchers should consider the following variants (Hatch 2002) in the information:

- Similarity in information that explains no variation in the contextual meanings.
- Differences in the expressions that indicate predictability in the contextual responses.
- Frequency of information, which indicates biasness unless it refers to a different context.
- Sequential information that explains continuous impact on related variables of the study.

- Correspondence of information that create interconnectivity of events, and
- Causation that explains as one effects appears to cause another.

The coding of information is required to develop an appropriate contents analysis plan, and perceive and interpret what is happening in the data by filtering the redundancy and biasness in the information. In live coding process, researchers keep the data rooted in the participant's own language, while the ethnographers employ descriptive coding to document and categorize the breadth of opinions stated by multiple participants. However, a social theorist may employ values coding to capture and label subjective perspectives. Coding is a heuristic process of discovering an exploratory problem-solving technique without mathematical formulas to follow. It is the initial step to analyze the qualitative information systematically. Coding is not just labeling, it is a process of linking variables to validate the research constructs. In qualitative inquiries such as case studies, ethnographic and phenomenological research, coding decisions affect the content analysis (Creswell 2007). Coding of information must be done by research proposition, constructs, and content categories to be analyzed. For example, in a social innovation research project, the hierarchical coding pattern can be planned in the following way:

- Community requirement
  - Code: Need
  - Code: Health
  - Code: Infrastructure
- Social innovation
  - Code: Accessibility
  - Code: Cost
  - Code: Type

The coding structure has two levels: domains and taxonomy. Domains are the broad dimensions of the research, whereas the taxonomy of codes represents the factors associated with the domains as discussed earlier in case of social innovation research. Some categories may contain clusters of coded data that merit further refinement into subcategories, which would help researchers to arrange the codes in thematic, conceptual, and theoretical domains for analyzing the contents.

In the coding process, the researcher must familiarize with the data and read the transcribed text to obtain the sense of the whole conversation. Later the narrations can be fragmented into smaller, meaning units. A meaning unit is the smallest unit that contains some of the insights into the researcher needs. These small meaning units can be phrases, or the constellation of sentences or paragraphs containing interrelated aspects of the narrations. In this process, each identified meaning unit is labeled with a code, which should be contextually understood to carry out the contents analysis (Graneheim and Lundman 2004). Coding in qualitative research is a dynamic process. Codes created inductively by the researchers by understanding the responses or drawing inferences, may change as the study progresses, and more data become available. Therefore, interpretations of the meaning units of codes that seem clear at the beginning might turn obscure during the process. Some of the qualitative data analysis software can fix the dynamic coding issue, but since computer programs are not embedded with the artificial intelligence to understand the verbal expressions and emotions, the human creativity is of importance.

Content Analysis

Content analysis in qualitative research is the most important step, which helps researchers draw appropriate inferences from the coded data, develop conclusions, and validate the grounded theory. It is a systematic approach to analyze information form the interviews, focus groups, opinion polls, open-ended survey, and text-data-mining outlets. A variety of strategies to categorize, compare, fragment, and integrate information can be used in content analysis. In addition, researchers can able to interpret several key trends, new social and economic values, and consumer perceptions based on the verbal and nonverbal information collected through research. To begin with the content analysis process, keywords need to be indexed under appropriate categories of the research, required for interpretation. The categorical separation of positive and negative perceptions emerging out the responses of subjects and researcher's observations facilitates systematic interpretation of the filtered information. The standard procedure of content analysis includes the following sequential stages:

- Coding/indexing
- Categorization
- Abstraction
- Comparison
- Defining dimensions of the data
- Triangulation and data integration
- Iteration
- Refutation (subjecting inferences to scrutiny)
- Interpretation (grasp of meaning, difficult to describe procedurally)

Besides coding/indexing and categorization discussed earlier, one of the challenges with the qualitative researchers is to prepare abstract of information acquired during the interview or field survey. Definition of keywords, and translation and description of the label are essential stages that determine the level of abstraction of data analysis and building of analytical themes. In analyzing the narrative information contents, language must be appropriately used as it impacts the quality of abstraction of theme(s). Recursive abstraction is a simple method based on summarizing the data in steps. It starts by summarizing a larger set of data (e.g., large text abstracted to $S1$), then summarizing the summarized portion (e.g., the abstracted $S1$ text to be summarized to $S2$) and so on, until a very focused and compact summary is reached close to accuracy and distinction. It is highly challenging for researchers to maintain precision in abstracting narrations of the broad-focused and open-ended qualitative inquiries. Upon completing the process of recursive abstraction, researcher can easily compare the text, re-assign codes, and draw inferences. Then researchers can develop broad dimensions of the data for constructing appropriate research propositions and refine the grounded theory of qualitative research (Hershkowitz, Schwarz, and Dreyfus 2001). By defining subsectors of inquiry on a broad theme, research dimensions can be added to stay more focused in carrying out content analysis. For example, in the qualitative inquiry on impact of social development, the sectoral dimensions of the social development can be created as health, education, housing, infrastructure and the like.

Most researchers blend qualitative and quantitative methods to examine different aspects of an overall research question. For example, they might use a randomized controlled trial to assess the effectiveness of a health care intervention through semi-structured interviews with patients and health professionals to consider the way the intervention practically affected the health conditions of the subjects. Data analysis is carried out in an integrated way to combine these findings and define this mixed analytical process as triangulation. In this process, the data sets for both methods are used separately by considering 3C's: appropriate convergence, complementarity, and consistency of the data. All care is taken to establish integration of findings from each method to ensure that the results offer total agreement (convergence), offer complementary information on the same issue (complementarity), and appear to be non-discrepant (consistency). The triangulation and data integration methods thus support each other to validate the qualitative inquiries of a large database (Farmer et al. 2006).

Iterative data refers to a systematic, repetitive, and recursive process in qualitative data analysis. This involves a sequence of tasks carried out in the same manner each time to extract the core contents and executed multiple times to refine the information (Mills, Durepos and Wiebe 2010). Iteration of narrations are the vigor of verbal and nonverbal expressions, which need to be coded and analyzed in the original form or by rationally modifying the text. Qualitative researchers also need to carefully examine the embedded meaning emerging out of the conversations, as the same idea embedded in the narration may be extended to contradictory explanations though there are sound arguments for a particular pattern. Such narrations need to be scrutinized to ensure whether they support or refute the analytical results (de Vaus 2009). Qualitative data can be interpreted appropriately after passing through all the stages of data analysis as discussed earlier.

Content analysis of qualitative information has changed over time from counting frequencies of critical words to a more interpretive approach. One of the principal challenges in analyzing the contents of qualitative inquiries is to differentiate between abstraction level and degree of flexibility in interpretation of contents spread across keywords, critical words, phrases, concepts, observations, and field notes. Analysis of qualitative contents helps to demonstrate inductive and deductive (epistemological) theories. In this process, the level of abstracting information and degree of interpretation are used in constructing categories, descriptive themes, and themes of meaning. However, unless the content analysis validates the grounded theory, its credibility and authenticity are always questionable (Graneheim, Lindgren, and Lundman 2017).

The contents analysis is carried out and interpreted in context to the research background, which may vary as political economic, technological, consumer behavior, market competition, and several other fields are dynamics. The thumb rule of analysis suggests that the qualitative research material should be analyzed systematically, variable-by-variable, question-by-question, or objective by objectives of the study to validate the predetermined research propositions. Following analytics procedure, researcher should divide the complete information into small content analytical units for categorical content analysis. The aspects of text interpretation following the research questions are put into categories, which have been carefully founded and revised within the process of analysis as feedback loops. The researcher should establish criteria of reliability and validity for qualifying the information in categorized variable segments.

Content analysis has three distinct approaches, which include conventional, directed, or summative methodologies. All three approaches are used to interpret meaning from the content of text data and, hence, adhere to the naturalistic paradigm. The major differences among these approaches are coding schemes, origins of codes, and threats to trustworthiness. In conventional content analysis, coding categories are derived directly from the text data. With a directed approach, analysis starts with a theory or relevant research findings as guidance for initial codes. A summative content analysis involves counting and comparisons, usually of keywords or content, followed by the interpretation of the underlying context (Hsieh and Shannon 2005).

Before taking up the content analysis, researchers must ensure that sources of the data are valid and reliable, and the coding categories are appropriately created, representing the data holistically. In addition, it is necessary to explore by observing the qualitative data whether the analysis can be generalized at the macro-, meso-, or micro-level. Accordingly, the contents analysis process can be scheduled by coding data, assessing the data reliability, and analyzing the results based on coding schemes. However, in the process of content analysis, it is important to eliminate perceptional biases and validate the interpretations across responses in the survey. In all types of analysis of qualitative data, regardless of whether it is within a positivist or naturalistic research tradition, the purpose of content analysis is to organize and elicit meaning from the data collected and draw realistic conclusions.

In a more liberal way, the content analysis can be used in both quantitative and qualitative methodologies in an inductive or a deductive way. For example, in a qualitative research study to measure the impact of media communications on social development, qualitative content analysis is predominant in social research, while quantitative content analysis can be conducted to measure the media effect. However, the researcher has to choose whether the analysis is to be a *manifest analysis* or a *latent analysis*. In a manifest analysis, the researcher describes verbatim what the informants actually say, stays very close to the text, uses the popular words of subjects, and describes them visible and obvious in the text. On the contrary, latent analysis is extended to an interpretive level where a researcher explores the underlying meaning of the text and draws implicit inferences (Bengtsson 2016).

Computer-Aided Qualitative Research

Computer-based analysis of qualitative information is growing over the manual processing of unorganized data. Researchers managing qualitative data analysis across disciplines increasingly face problems in handling narrations and text-data-mining processing. Consequently, there is a growing literature on computer-assisted qualitative data analysis software (CAQDAS). Various software such as NVivo, Atlas.ti, and MAXQDA emerged as commercial off-the-shelf technologies, evolved over time from pioneering programmable software development industry during the 1980s, and became available for public use within a decade. Other software to assist the qualitative research analysis include QDA Miner, Dedoose, and HyperRESEARCH. These computer-aided qualitative research tools helped the researchers enhance their ability to search, categorize, examine, and develop identifiable content analysis patterns in each specific research in large data sets. Working with the computer-aided software, researchers benefit the following functions to carry out skillfully:

- Organize qualitative data.
- Manage fragmented qualitative data.
- Create memos identifying initial thoughts.
- Organize field notes and observations of researcher.
- Assign codes to qualitative data.
- Combining and assemble codes under multi-layer categories or themes.
- Generate word, phrases frequency searches, and develop semantic map.
- Conducting content analysis.
- Create mind maps to organize perceptions of subjects and researcher's concepts.

The previously stated software for qualitative data analysis allows researchers to upload text documents to a new project, which can be titled for each observation, and initiate the coding and data analysis process. Some CAQDAS only use text, whereas others can import images, audio and video data, newspaper clippings, and books. The software systems also have the capability to auto-define and organize coding and text information, and analyze relationships across the coded variables and predetermined themes in the data sets. Some of the available software packages with these features include Ethnograph, Atlas Ti, NVivo, and Qualrus. The use of software for qualitative research prompts researchers to analyze simultaneous contents and examine multilayer data set with computer-assisted arraying patterns to conduct systematic analysis. In this manner, the scientific rigor of qualitative research is enhanced, and an audit trail is created about the actions performed by the software. However, the debate on CAQDAS is bidirectional to explain the merits and demerits of computer-aided analysis for qualitative data. While using the software, a trail of analysis needs to be preserved to replicate the research and develop transparency in content analysis (Conrad and Reinharz 1984). Many software systems support retrievals, and searches on data can be repeated in a consistent way, which enables researchers to conduct retrospective checks to ascertain whether the analysis is streamlined (Fielding and Lee 1998). However, it has often argued that an audit trail computer-aided data analytics is not always automatic and still requires systematic and structured record keeping by the researchers (Miles and Huberman 1994).

One of the advantages of CAQDAS is that it enables the researcher to focus on analytical techniques, enhancing intellectual thoughts in developing data interpretation, and drawing appropriate inferences, rather than engaging in manual tasks. However, the major underlying problem with the usage of software for qualitative information analysis is that implicit assumptions of the software architecture interferes with the qualitative research process, and results in corrupting the expressions, meaning and interpretation that the qualitative data bring with manual analysis process (Rodik and Primorac 2015).

Some software such as "Atlas.ti" appears to be a powerful workbench for qualitative data analysis, particularly for large sections of text, visual, and audio data. This software offers support to the researchers to analyze and interpret text using coding and annotating activities during data analysis process. Software that have applications for comprehensive analysis benefit researchers in several ways right from data collection process to reporting stage. Using the software, researchers can search for similarities and differences in narrations, transcript texts, codes and categories, themes, concepts, and manage continuous process of information input and output analysis. Content analysis commences with reading all the data and then dividing the data into smaller more meaningful units. In the qualitative research, data segments are organized into a system that is predominantly derived from the data, which implies that the analysis is inductive. The CAQDAS help researchers to map comparisons to build and refine categories, define conceptual similarities, and to discover new patterns of responses.

Some sociological researchers have used the CAQDAS as a tool for conversation analysis (CA). The application of CA through computer-aided software have been expanded to research in the areas of anthropology, communication, and linguistics. The advancement of research technology in social sciences and computer sciences has proved to provide testament to the robust findings of earlier studies using CA methodology growth for five decades (Kasper and Wagner 2014). Over time, the "applied conversation analysis" is conducted in many areas and types of studies beyond social sciences such as clinical qualitative studies and macro-societal issues (Antaki 2011).

The debate on CAQDAS brought several application issues about the reliability of results to the surface. However, software programmers and many qualitative researchers saw the benefits and potential of using software for analyzing qualitative data, but there remained difference in opinions, as software cannot substitute the human elements in describing the emotions, perceptions, and latent thoughts, which constitute the part of qualitative information.

Summary

Several perspectives and challenges in managing qualitative information have been discussed in this chapter. Management of qualitative data is often difficult, as often researchers are not aware of the expected volume of information despite the sample population of subjects being specified. Proper data management is necessary to maintain the security of the data for conducting meta-analysis and data interpretations in the longitudinal studies. Qualitative data management needs confidentiality to protect the information of subjects and professional commitment to the participants in the qualitative inquiry process. Acquiring information through qualitative instruments, analyzing content, and drawing inferences is a scientific approach while blending such inferences with informal observations, filed notes, and public views is an art in qualitative research, as it needs a rationale and community sensitive vision.

Collecting information during qualitative inquiries provides ample scope of acquiring comprehensive data to conduct multilayered content analysis. However, mismanagement of data causes nonretrieval and redundancy problems. Besides the mechanical approaches to store and retrieve the data, researchers also need to manage subjects in retrieving the information. Researchers must understand the cognitive ecosystem of subjects, and manage the information emerging from conscious mind and stored in the subconscious memories. The content analysis of descriptive information needs to be done spanning from macro to micro perspectives. Research questions can be broadly classified into three categories: conceptual, problem-based, and knowledge-driven perspectives.

Qualitative researchers often face metaphoric expressions of subjects while responding to the interview questions. Sensory cognition and episodic memories facilitate the cognitive analysis of information. Transcription is necessary for open-ended responses, information of focus groups, observation, spoken language and slang expressions, and individual interviews.

Data coding, defined as a field information identification tag, is a necessary step in qualitative research, which facilitates researchers to carry out systematic information analysis. A code in qualitative inquiry is most often a set of alphanumeric fields or short phrases. The coding of information is required to develop an appropriate contents analysis plan to perceive and interpret information. It is a systematic approach to analyze information form the interviews, focus groups, opinion polls, open-ended survey, and text-data-mining outlets. A variety of strategies to categorize, compare, fragment, and integrate information can be used in content analysis. Content analysis has three distinct approaches, which include conventional, directed, or summative methodologies.

Though the computer-based analysis of qualitative information is growing over the manual processing of unorganized data, researchers managing qualitative data analysis across disciplines increasingly face problems in handling narrations and text-data-mining processing.

References

Antaki, C. 2011. *Applied Conversation Analysis*. Basingstoke: Palgrave Macmillan.

Arora, R., and C. Stoner. 2009. "A Mixed Method Approach to Understanding Brand Personality." *Journal of Product & Brand Management* 18, no. 4, pp. 272–83.

Banner, D.J., and J.W. Albarran. 2009. "Computer-assisted Qualitative Data Analysis Software: A Review." *Canadian Journal of Cardiovascular Nursing* 19, no. 3, pp. 24–27.

Bengtsson, M. 2016. "How to Plan and Perform a Qualitative Study Using Content Analysis. *Nursing Plus Open* 2, no. 1, pp. 8–14.

Conrad, P., and S. Reinharz. 1984. "CAQDAS Software and Qualitative Data: Editors Introductory Essay." *Qualitative Sociology* 7, nos. 1/2, pp. 3–15.

Creswell, J.W. 2005. *Educational Research: Planning, Conducting, and Evaluating Quantitative and Qualitative Research*. Upper Saddle River, New Jersey: Pearson Education.

Creswell, J.W. 2007. *Qualitative Inquiry and Research Design: Choosing Among Five Traditions*. Thousand Oaks, CA: Sage.

Danes, J.E., J.S. Hess, J.W. Story, and J.L. York. 2010. "Brand Image Associations for Large Virtual Groups." *Qualitative Market Research: An International Journal* 13, no. 3, pp. 309–23.

de Vaus, D. 2009. *Research Design in Social Research*. Thousand Oaks, CA: Sage.

Farmer, T., K. Robinson, S.J. Elliott, and J. Eyles. 2006. "Developing and Implementing a Triangulation Protocol for Qualitative Health Research." *Qualitative Health Research* 16, no. 3, pp. 377–94.

Fielding, N.G., and R.M. Lee. 1998. *Computer Analysis and Qualitative Research*. London Sage.

Graneheim, U.H., and B. Lundman. 2004. "Qualitative Content Analysis in Nursing Research: Concepts, Procedures and Measure to Achieve Trustworthiness." *Nurse Education Today* 24, no. 1, pp. 105–12.

Graneheim, U.H., B.M. Lindgren, and B. Lundman. 2017. "Methodological Challenges in Qualitative Content Analysis: A Discussion Paper." *Nurse Education Today* 56, no. 1, pp. 29–34.

Halcomb, E.J., and P.M. Davidson. 2006. "Is Verbatim Transcription of Interview Data Always Necessary?" *Applied Nursing Research* 19, no. 1, pp. 38–42.

Hardy, L.J., A. Hughes, E. Hulen, and A.L. Schwartz. 2016. "Implementing Qualitative Data Management Plans to Ensure Ethical Standards in Multi-partner Centers." *Journal of Empirical Research on Human Research Ethics* 11, no. 2, pp. 191–98.

Hatch, A.J. 2002. *Doing Qualitative Research in Education Setting*. New York, NY: State University of New York Press.

Hershkowitz, R., B.B. Schwarz, and T. Dreyfus. 2001. "Abstraction in Context: Epistemic Actions." *Journal for Research in Mathematics Education* 32, no. 2, pp. 195–222.

Hooper, C.S. 2011. "Qualitative in Context." *Journal of Advertising Research* 51, pp. 163–66.

Kasper, G., and J. Wagner. 2014. "Conversation Analysis in Applied Linguistics." *Annual Review of Applied Linguistics* 34, no. 1, pp. 171–212.

Levine, H.G. 1985. "Principles of Data Storage and Retrieval for Use in Qualitative Evaluations." *Educational Evaluation and Policy Analysis* 7, no. 2, pp. 169–86.

Lin, L.C. 2009. "Data Management and Security in Qualitative Research." *Dimensions of Critical Care Nursing* 28, no. 3, pp. 132–37.

MacQueen, K.M., and B. Milstein. 1999. "A Systems Approach to Qualitative Data Management and Analysis." *Field Methods* 11, no. 1, pp. 27–39.

Manderson, L., M. Kelaher, and N. Woelz-Stirling. 2001. "Developing Qualitative Databases for Multiple Users." *Qualitative Health Research* 11, no. 2, pp. 149–60.

Mesulam, M.M. 1998. "From Sensation to Cognition." *Brain* 121, no. 6, pp. 1013–52.

Miles, M.B., and A.M. Huberman. 1994. *Qualitative Data Analysis: A Sourcebook of New Methods.* Beverly Hills, CA: Sage.

Mills, A.J., G. Durepos, and E. Wiebe. 2010. *Encyclopedia of Case Study Research.* Thousand Oaks, CA: Sage.

Pinch, W.J.E. 2000. "Confidentiality: Concept Analysis and Clinical Application." *Nursing Forum* 35, no. 2, pp. 5–16.

Rodik, P., and J. Primorac. 2015. "To Use or Not to Use: Computer-Assisted Qualitative Data Analysis Software Usage among Early-Career Sociologists in Croatia." *Forum: Qualitative Social Research* 16, no. 1, p. Art. 12.

Rosciano, A. 2015. "The Effectiveness of Mind Mapping as an Active Learning Strategy Among Associate Degree Nursing Students." *Teaching and Learning in Nursing* 10, no. 2, pp. 93–99.

Wheeler, M.E., and E.J. Ploran. 2009. "Episodic Memory." In *Encyclopedia of Neuroscience,* ed. L.R. Squire, 1167–72. Cambridge, MA: Academic Press.

Woogara, J. 2015. "Patients' Privacy of the Person and Human Rights." *Nursing Ethics* 12, no. 3, pp. 273–87.

CHAPTER 4

Evidence-Based Research

Overview

Evidence-based research is one of the most used methodologies in qualitative research across disciplines from social sciences to medicine and health care. Qualitative research based on cognitive and community-led evidences provides small, but profoundly significant, proofs in social, cultural, and entrepreneurial development emerging from governmental and organizational interventions. This chapter addresses the contemporary trends in evidence-based qualitative research in addition to community-driven methodologies in qualitative research. Action research is another qualitative methodology developed and implemented in social and ethnological perspectives. This chapter defines action research as social development projects are networked around various human elements. In addition, participatory research appraisal, case research, focus group administration, and anthropomorphic research studies as extended evidence-based qualitative research designs are discussed in this chapter. Complexity of information loops is not uncommon in qualitative inquiries. Information loops during information acquisition process occur due to unclear presentation of questions to the subjects. Contextual discussions on qualitative loops analysis has been presented in this chapter. This chapter also highlights theoretical aspects of reasoned action and differential strategies.

Qualitative research has several touch points like liberal narrations, storytelling, retrieval of memories, and text-data-mining. However, information acquired through each mode needs to be validated through appropriate evidence. This task often turns the qualitative research process into a complex one and makes it ambiguous without tangible proofs that can validate the narrations of the subjects. The pursuit of evidence-based qualitative research implies a move beyond individual opinions and lays greater focus on the organization and management systems that fall with the research study. For example, while conducting qualitative research on social health care marketing, researchers need to move beyond acquiring information from the beneficiaries and collect evidences from the various role players such government and community health care teams, service delivery systems, service settings, and packages of social health care. More opinions need to be collected for exploring effective ways of managing change within systems, and at the level of individual professionals. Qualitative research extended to the organizational perspective in each research projects would help researchers to document evidence for validating the individual opinions (Black 1994).

Qualitative evidence is the true measures of data interpretation in empirical research unlike quantitative figures. Qualitative research often involves vague measurements to validate the information acquired from the subjects using words and phrases such as "a lot," "a little," "many," "most." However, the strength of content analysis can be enhanced by presenting the quantified statements against the open-ended narrations. Such evidence-based qualitative research can be defined as cautious positivism. Qualitative evaluations can identify small but profoundly significant evidences in social, cultural, and entrepreneurial developments resulting from governmental and organizational interventions. These small evidences can be images, videos, or documents, which can be integrated into the content analysis. A good qualitative research resists examining the views of those being researched merely through the unstructured instrument but tends to document the interrelated facts from different public sources. While documenting evidences, the qualitative researchers should be able to explain how different sources of knowledge about the same issue can be compared and contrasted. In the absence of public evidence, it is necessary for the researchers to validate whether the subjective perceptions and experiences analyzed in the study can be treated as knowledge in their own right (Popay and Williams 1998).

Qualitative data analysis is often challenged, as it is not a stand-alone methodological approach to the opinion analysis of subjects on various social, anthropological, ethnographic, and cognitive studies. A study design depends on the nature of the research problem, its conceptual and theoretical framework, and the quality of information collected. Thus, narrative analysis supported by the imagery or documented evidence would be able to authenticate the results and the possibility of its generalization. Information analysis needs validation because most qualitative studies use self-explanatory common knowledge or even intuitive phases. Many qualitative studies restrict the explanation of data analysis to the phrase "categories and themes emerged from the data," or invoke mention of a computer package that has been used to manage the data. This is a prevailing issue in the qualitative research, which often jeopardizes the study due to lack of clarity in expressions. Hence, there exists the demand for tangible evidence to support the information analysis and conclusions of the study (Green et al. 2007).

Research-based practice program like social laboratories, action research programs, and community health care system provide a systematic, participative approach to the design, implementation, and evaluation of evidence-based practice guidelines for the qualitative researchers. Evidence in qualitative research studies can also help to shape and clarify key questions by informing the interventions, comparisons, and organizational outcomes that each response should focus on. For example, subjects cite their experiences upon reviewing the existing social developments, the benefits of community health projects, or the benefits of consumer products marketing programs initiated by the companies as compared to the projected measures. Acceptability of a social innovation, co-created business initiatives, or development intervention toward creating value to stakeholders can be defined as organizational or community evidence to support the opinion of stakeholders. The guideline to document the evidence lies in the process of cause, action, and effect performed through a systematic process. The stages and gates (review points) in a consumer marketing, social marketing, or community development programs provide the scope to conduct an evidence-based qualitative research. Qualitative evidence synthesis offers a schematic platform for measuring and validating attitudes, beliefs and feelings of the subjects interviewed in the qualitative research. Systematic evidence can be synthesized against isolated findings by integrating the multilayered views from longitudinal studies (Dalton et al. 2017). Therefore, evidence-based decision-making is becoming increasingly important in many diverse domains, which has created the need for improved tools to aggregate evidence from multiple sources in qualitative research. For instance, in consumer products marketing, much valuable evidence emerges in the form of the concept test of products, and prototype trials that compare the relative merits of consumer satisfaction.

Evidence-based qualitative research sometimes fails to analyze the cognitive perceptions of consumers, as emotion-led responses are largely subjective. When researchers get involved with emotions of the consumers, the perceptions revealed by the subjects can be complex. Qualitative consumer research is regarded more as an art than science. However, evidence on qualitative perspectives of consumers can be analyzed by listing the emotional lexicon from initial inquiries and reviewing previous studies. Big Data analytics is also linked to specific consumer behaviors and loyalty programs. Most of the consumer product companies identify and leverage the specific motivators that maximize their competitive advantage, and such qualitative information analysis can be used in consumer-centric growth. Evidence-based qualitative research process helps in mapping the consumer perceptions, emotions, attitudes, and behavior across time and geo-demographic segments. Researchers should thoroughly review the existing consumer research and customer insight data and look for qualitative descriptions of what motivates the consumers' need, desire, and expectations. The lexicons on emotions and motivations should be documented during qualitative enquiries and explained by the researchers as evidence in support of expressions. Such documentation provides a guideline to map the emotions and explain the association of consumers with the products, brands, and companies (Magids, Zorfas, and Leemon 2015).

Action Research

Qualitative research on ethnological and social perspectives, and clinical and social preventive medicine has been historically leading to developmental concerns through the action research programs, which enables researchers to participate in implementation of evidence-based research recommendations. In business today, most consumer-centric companies have also adapted to the action research process in implementing the suggestions emerging out of the qualitative research on consumer emotions,

motivational factors, value perspectives based on the satisfaction measures. Companies accordingly organize action research laboratories focusing on society in general and consumers in particular. Action research
educates the researchers and their sponsors on how the subjects of the
research interpret their own behavior rather than imposing a theory from
outside. It considers that context is as important as the actions it studies,
and attempts to represent the totality of the social, cultural, and economic
situation (Reason and Bradbury 2001). In planning action research as an
extended part of the qualitative research, the research agenda must be set
following the sequential stages suggested as follows:

- Data collection of the existing social and business situation
  from records, previous studies, and interviews with experts,
  using participatory maps and flowcharts to document the flow
  opinions of subject and expertise, cause-and-effect relationships, and organizational interactions.
- Identification of action research projects in the social, ethnological, or business area by interviews with local businesses
  and social development leaders.
- Mapping of attributes of identified action research projects
  using chart key infrastructure, inputs and support services,
  action research players, and constructing the value chain for
  implementing the project.
- Identifying the participating business, governmental, and
  public institutions, rules, norms and trends of the market
  environment.
- Developing a stage-gate process of action research by identifying the tools and techniques of data collection, analysis, linking suggestions to the goals and objectives of action research,
  identifying implementation phases, and founding gates. Gates
  need to the clearly labeled with the quality checks, social and
  business reviews, and the work breakdown phases.
- Analysis of collected data can be conducted by using data display and reduction techniques for qualitative data to identify
  main themes and trends. Supplementing descriptive statistics
  for data to comprehend qualitative information.

- Implementing the action research points, reviewing results, drawing inferences, and drawing conclusions.

The action research projects developed and implemented in the social and ethnological perspectives are commonly defined as social development projects driven on the human elements. The action research projects promoted by the companies are largely seen as corporate social responsibility projects aimed to benefit stakeholders and society. Such projects are strategically planned and continue for long time alike the social development projects. The popular methodology action research is shown in the Figure 4.1.

The action research guidelines described in Figure 4.1 explain three major dimensions: methodological, technical, and practical. Action research projects are built on the predetermined grounded theory, based on which the research propositions for action research are developed. The study design of action research includes determining data collection tools and determining causes and effects. The project charter is developed accordingly, and information is collected on several principal and intervening variables by empowering the subjects and role players associated with the action research. In order to conduct longitudinal action research projects, work stations are established across geographic destinations. Researchers conduct brainstorming sessions in teams to map the concepts and action points for implementation.

As action research is derived from qualitative research design, it is implemented using a participatory methodology by involving subjects and project role players. In action research projects, teams of participants are constituted with the allocation of tasks within the predetermined research domains. Participants derive causal maps for action research to express their views on the cause and effect, and the strategic perspectives of the project. Maps are prepared on convenient platforms with identifying tags using colors. In social development and ethnological research, rural participants draw concept and action maps on the ground using various natural indicators like stones, flowers, leaves, and the like. Concept maps represent the existing situation and the expected development based on grounded theory built during the initial qualitative research. By developing these maps, and participating in brainstorming sessions

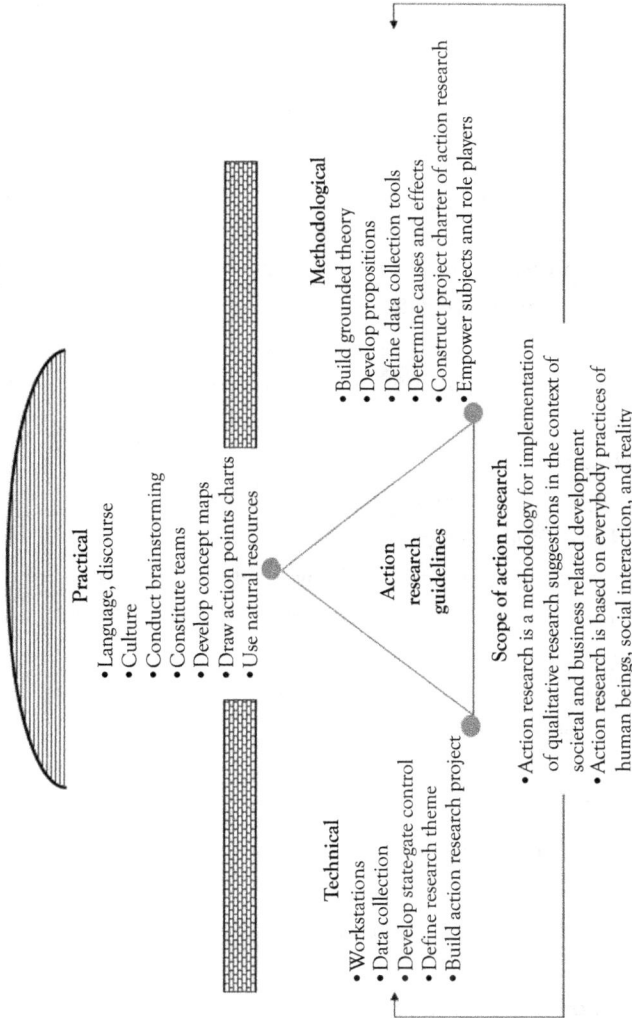

Practical
- Language, discourse
- Culture
- Conduct brainstorming
- Constitute teams
- Develop concept maps
- Draw action points charts
- Use natural resources

Methodological
- Build grounded theory
- Develop propositions
- Define data collection tools
- Determine causes and effects
- Construct project charter of action research
- Empower subjects and role players

Technical
- Workstations
- Data collection
- Develop state-gate control
- Define research theme
- Build action research project

Action research guidelines

Scope of action research
- Action research is a methodology for implementation of qualitative research suggestions in the context of societal and business related development
- Action research is based on everybody practices of human beings, social interaction, and reality

Figure 4.1 Pathway of conducting action research

and thematic focus groups, subjects demonstrate their perceptions on the maps drawn. The perceptual maps are subsequently adjusted to reflect the action points associated with the objectives of research and implementation. Accordingly, thematic clusters are developed and subsequently adjusted to reflect the peer judgments about how these strategic issues can be resolved. The mapping exercise results in the creation of a group causal map where new clusters emerge by evaluating the external factors. The concept and action maps developed by the action research participants help researchers to continuously discuss and refine issues, prioritize actions, find means and ends for effective execution of actions, and then progress with the action research projects (e.g., Eden and Ackermann 2018). Broad areas, methodology, and approaches to carry out analysis and findings are summarized as follows:

- Common areas of action research projects
  - Family, society, political subjects, governance, impact studies
- Theory-led methodology
  - Naturalistic-interpretive (involvement)
  - Constructivist-problem-solving (analytical and strategic)
  - Pragmatic philosophy-historicity (documentary, spatial, and temporal)
- Popular approaches to carry out analysis and findings in action research projects
  - Observations
  - In-depth interviews (representative)
  - Public poll analysis
  - Ideographic (derived meaning)
  - Nomothetic (generalization)

Participatory action research is an effective method of actively guiding and engaging the qualitative research teams in a reflective and collaborative research practice to implement the emerging results on the social, ethnographic, and business-related developmental actions. In the process of action research, participants and researchers learn to conduct applied interviews and need assessments and gain confidence to build rapport with the social or business stakeholders (Hickey, et al. 2018). Action research is an iterative process involving action, reflection, theory, and practice (Brydon-Miller, Greenwood, and Maguire 2003). Action research projects are specific to the stakeholder needs and possess developmental orientation because research informs practice and practice informs research (Avison, Lau, Myers, and Nielsen 1999).

Participatory Research Appraisal

Participatory research appraisal (PRA) is a qualitative approach used to plan action research projects. This approach is based on community participation to document the knowledge and opinions of subjects in planning social and business development projects and programs. PRA engages the total population, irrespective of a defined sample size to develop concept maps and action research plans. Since PRA is a community-based research approach, it tends to eliminate the individual biases and validate the populist opinions. In this research approach, cognitive appraisal of the subjects is situational and is shared across members of the community in the study area. Action research, therefore, leads to the developmental activities that are creative, productive, and sustainable over a period. Action research evolves through participatory learning methods (PALM) to implement the suggested action plan.

PRA methodology is described as a social learning tool with the growing family of approaches and methods that enable people within the community to share, enhance, and analyze their knowledge and living conditions to plan and to act. PRA has evolved within the social research and ethnographic methods in social sciences. This approach embeds direct learning from local people offsetting biases, optimizing opinion trade-offs, triangulating information, and seeking diversity. In the PRA study, design researchers can facilitate content analysis in two phases: by the subjects (unfiltered) and systematically using coding and analysis (filtered). The subjects in the PRA process should be able to ensure critical self-awareness and responsibility and share the true and contextual (evidence-based) information with the researchers. The major attributes of PRA are as follows:

- Evidence mapping and interpretation
- Socio-cultural considerations in field work design
- Individuals vs society, content analysis of qualitative research, triangulation
- Styles of participation and observation, and
- Ethics in field research: conduct of investigator and subjects of the study.

The advanced methods of PRA allow subjects to practice participatory mapping and modeling, transect walks, and matrix scoring. In PRA exercise, subject also work on mapping their well-being grouping, and ranking community amenities and infrastructure. The subjects in the PRA process also express the existing gaps and future plans. Research also motivates subjects to develop institutional diagrams indicating the institutions involved in the development projects, their role, and performance. Such institutional diagrams are useful in analyzing the perceptions of people not only for social development project, but also to evaluate the corporate social responsibility projects. In addition, PRA encourages subjects to develop seasonal calendars, trend, and change analysis, and suggest pathways of information analysis. In the PRA investigation, sharing and analysis are open-ended and often visual to society in general and the subjects in particular through comparisons across spatial and temporal dimensions.

The PRA methodology has been widely used to explore business opportunities in rural or bottom-of-the-pyramid geodemographic segments. The participatory research has been useful in exploring the ways in which businesses use and create diverse forms of rural and social capital. PRA methodology helps entrepreneurs describe the attributes of manufacturers, marketers, and consumers distinctively in the small businesses. Therefore, PRA triggers the debate about whether location alone is a sufficient parameter for defining rural-ness and understanding the dynamics of social change driven by local business development (Bosworth and Turner 2018). An effective participatory appraisal requires greater empowerment of the subjects. In general, sometimes the information paths are complex and chronologically discrete in PRA compared to the other qualitative research methods and tools. Therefore, it is not possible to establish standardized methods and tools in PRA, because each process of participatory research must be tailored for the specific community where subjects express their views and construct maps (Menconi, Grohmann, and Mancinelli 2017).

Besides concept and action mapping, PRA adapts to the common qualitative research tools such as semistructured interviewing and focus groups. PRA applications include natural resources management, agriculture, poverty and social programs, and health and food security. The participatory research method can be used to develop matrix scoring for varieties of social indicators like income, education, employment, health, consumption culture. The matrix drawn by the subjects with the help of PRA researchers provides fascinating and useful information and insights, and good-looking tables with diagrams derived by the subjects (Chambers 1994). Sharing knowledge, experience, and opinions of the subjects take three main forms:

- Subjects initially brainstorm and share knowledge among themselves by analyzing the responses in groups and develop concept maps using visual indicators in a natural setting.
- Subjects then share information with the researchers.
  As a condition for facilitating this process, researchers or community anchors clarify doubts, explain the purpose of the research, and restrain themselves from putting forward their own ideas over the prevailing reality in the study area.
- Researchers learn from each other and maintain field diary with their observation to complement the content analysis.

Applied and grassroots qualitative research has contributed to the PRA momentum. This methodology has usually proved enjoyable and has generated rapport among researchers, subjects, and community in general. Information and insights emerging from the PRA exercise are often diverse, detailed, complex, interesting and useful, which are shared in a short time. Hence, the PRA qualitative methodology has proved to be both powerful and popular.

One of the best examples of PRA-led development is the Self-Employed Women's Association (SEWA), a women's trade union started by women workers in Gujarat, India, in 1972. The organization conducts

PRA exercises with rural women to learn the current socioeconomic conditions, their expectations toward improving the quality of life, economic status, and family earnings. SEWA supports formation of member-based organizations of poor working women, and put them in business, manufacturing and marketing activities. The first such organization was SEWA Bank, followed by diverse cooperatives and producer groups of women with livelihoods as artisans, milk producers, and farmers. Later on, women formed service cooperatives like those around health and child care. Since 2013, SEWA has provided energy solutions to communities with little or no access to energy. Energy is a critical input for women in the informal sector, both for quality of life and economic mobility.

Case Research

Case research is a narrative analysis of a given social or business-related problem, which is explained with a protagonist. A business case study is essentially a story about a problem, challenge, or opportunity faced by a manager or stakeholders. A case research can be conducted using qualitative tools and techniques. A decision maker and a few stakeholders are aligned with in-depth interviews to share their opinion on a predetermined research theme. Contents of a case study including narrative details, direct quotations from those involved in the events of the case, and opinions form the basis for an analytic discussion in the case research. The case research has been defined in several ways, prominently as an investigation on the existing situations. Robson (2005) identifies case research as a strategy used to explore and explain a given situation in business or society using multiple sources of evidence, while Yin (2003) expresses that it is an inquiry to document phenomenological perspectives through qualitative research. Narrations and storyboards enrich the case research process. Case research involves gathering of information from some entities such as people, groups, or organizations on the qualitative approaches, which lacks in experimental control (Benbasat, Goldstein, and Mead 1987).

Qualitative case research methodology provides tools to study complex phenomena within social and business contexts. Case research is also useful in building inductive theory, evaluating development programs and projects, and developing action-based interventions. Case research includes writing the research questions, developing propositions, determining the attributes of the case under study, binding the case, and a discussion of data sources and triangulation (Baxter and Jack 2008). Though case research is a part of wider qualitative inquiries, it has many complexities. Interpretive approach in qualitative studies commonly faces problems of fluidity and flexibility of the research process, use of contextual basis for research questions and research method, and multidimensional narrations, and interpretation of the contents. However, a case study is considered to be parallel with the field study and observational study, each focusing on different aspects of the qualitative research methodology. All case studies developed using qualitative research methodology do not generate the same results on causal relationships like controlled experiments. However, they provide deeper understanding of facts in an ethnographic study. Case studies have been criticized for being of less value as they cannot be generalized and remain as just a research reference (Runeson and Höst 2009). In developing case research, the following points need to be considered by every researcher:

- Case environment
  - Market, organization, consumers, governance
- Case plot
  - Objective(s), the crux, and the focus
- Case players
  - The anchor, supporting cast, intervening roles, and pacifiers
- Case information
  - Strategies, statistics, semantics (logic), and synergy (interaction)
- Case description
  - Narrative, progressive, negative, realistic
- Case conclusion
  - Abrupt, futuristic, indecisive

Researchers need to assess the case study environment by determining the discussion stream related to market, organization, consumers, or social governance. Accordingly, the objectives of case research need to be developed in context of the problem to be addressed. The role of the protagonist, decision-maker, and other role players in the case need to be clearly set in the discussion, with the support of evidence, narrations, semantics, and synergy. Case study methodology has been intuitively developed for exploratory research and some researchers still limit case studies for this purpose (Flyvbjerg 2007). Nonetheless, case studies are also extended to conduct descriptive research like consumer behavior, ethnic and cultural effects on business, and community development, which need to be discussed case-by-case with the generalization of results. Case studies may also be used for testing the existing theories in confirmatory studies (Andersson and Runeson 2007).

Case research is popularly used in ethnographic studies as the major research methodology to explore the problems associated with the human elements in society, business, and governance. Ethnographic study is a specialized type of case research with focus on cultural practices or longitudinal studies with large amounts of participant–observer data and narrations of subjects. A case study can also be integrated with other research methods, for example, a survey, literature search, or archival analyses may be part of its data collection. Ethnographic methods, like interviews and observations, are mostly used for data collection in case studies (Robinson, Segal, and Sharp 2007). Case research is often large, as narrations and information might be repetitive, complex, and biased. As the information is based on qualitative data, it cannot be presented in condensed form in tables, diagrams, and statistical results unlike quantitative data. Qualitative analyses are not based on statistical significance and cannot be interpreted in terms of a probability or temporal projections. However, reasoning and linking of observations lead to conclusions in the case research, which can also be subjectively interpreted.

Qualitative case research must be conducted systematically and rigorously, and should be accountable for its quality and its claims. It should be strategically conducted with flexible research design and should be contextual to the predetermined objectives. Essentially, this means that qualitative researchers should make decisions by developing a sound research design and stay sensitive to the changing contexts in which the research takes place and to the ecosystem of qualitative research comprising the study area, respondents, questionnaire, and code of ethics. Qualitative research should involve critical self-scrutiny of information or exhibit active reflexivity during data collection process. Accordingly, researchers should constantly take stock of their actions, informant's attitude and their role in the research process, and refine the information acquisition modalities accordingly. However, at times, a researcher cannot be neutral, or objective, or detached, from the knowledge and evidence that are being generated during data collection process. Researchers conducting qualitative studies should seek to understand their role in the process, stay proactive, interactive, and reactive, and exhibit reflexivity to moderate the qualitative responses.

A researcher must be truly interested in, and passionate about, the case research to be conducted, and should get involved in managing open discussions with the protagonist and other role-players of the case. Such involvement of investigator helps in setting the scenario for managing narrations and information acquisition by creating adequate interest among the respondents. Thoroughness of researchers on the subject can fill a knowledge gap among respondents, drive respondents to follow through the research process, and stay close to the research goals (Farber 2006). Research questions are not the same questions that are presented during the process of interviewing participants within the study. They are the most important facets within the qualitative study and should be open-ended at large. Most qualitative researches are inductive in nature and allow the researcher to generate research propositions from analysis of the collected data. The questions supporting the research propositions are one of the distinguishing factors between qualitative research and quantitative research. Upon reviewing the previous qualitative studies, research propositions are formed based on the research data to confirm or reject preconceived notions, relationships, or correlations (Burck 2005). A researcher must develop skills that enable him to gain trust with the participant being interviewed. Qualitative research questions should be open-ended also to help investigator to stay with an open mind. These questions guide the research study, and at the same time, allow subquestions and incepting questions to pave the way for new and emerging questions (Ohman 2005).

Language is an important cultural tool for effectively conducting international business in the host countries. Language has a deep-rooted sentiment in people. It is not just a spoken word, but also symbolic communication of time, space, things, friendship, and agreements. The language people speak is part of the culture in which they are raised. Therefore, the language used in all marketing communications including advertising, public relations, and general communications should reflect the unique cultural expressions and values of the target locale. Non-verbal communication occurs through gestures, expressions, and other body movements.

Market research firms provide solution to the multinational companies through qualitative case research studies by conducting trade surveys on who the respondents should be, when to administer the questionnaires, what should be the nature of questions, and the number of questions to be used in the trade surveys. These market research firms provide a good starting point for further data gathering and analysis. Market research also involves *direct observation* on customers who are buying and using the products. This method enables companies to know the consumer behavior toward existing products and develop competitive marketing strategy accordingly. The behavior of consumers toward the existing products gives important clues to customer preferences, especially in mature markets. In markets, where access is free and the customers have well-developed preferences, the sales records of various products constitute a shortcut to understanding customer preferences. This method is very useful during the prelaunch stage for the foreign firms to develop an appropriate launch of their products in the segmented markets. The method of observation also faces some practical difficulties if certain assumptions are made to interpret the observed issues. A firm may assume that existing products reflect customer preferences, and such assumption is likely to hold only in mature markets with no entry barriers. However, in markets where customers have been deprived of products because of trade barriers, consumer preferences might well display a desire for something different. Such latent preferences cannot be uncovered through observation. On the other hand, *causal marketing research* is sometimes combined with experimental methods of research and causal models (Rajagopal 2018). The aim of such research may be to determine the extent to which a causal variable such as price or advertising affects variables such as brand preference or purchase. There are typical research designs that may be used in such experimental methods to estimate and validate causal business models. The problems addressed in the casual market researches tend to be about the fine-tuning of price levels, testing of alternative advertising copy and visuals, and the link between postsales service and customer satisfaction. The basic notion underlying the research is that a multinational company needs to understand precisely which of the contemplated marketing activities will have an appropriate bearing on the results.

Observation and narratives approach is commonly used in case research for formulating descriptive marketing research plans. Focus group and participatory approaches are useful exercises for exploratory marketing research. The survey method has proved to be an effective research approach in exploratory studies for analyzing data. This makes use of quantitative methods leading to a distinctive analysis of factors and future projections. This approach is identified as one of the most scientific methods in relating a research approach with its results. However, a good marketing research approach needs to possess the following qualities:

- Scientific method
- Originality and creativity
- Potential to use multiple methods for cross checking the emerging results
- Interdependence on analytical models and data sets
- Cost of research

A marketing research plan should comprise the aforementioned qualities for drawing effective results, and for preparing a useful document to be used for optimizing business propositions in and any situation.

Market research is an important tool for companies in the emerging markets to develop appropriate strategies for stakeholders, suppliers, and alliance partners. The emerging markets of developing countries have received signals from global competition and are rising fast. However, there are many hidden complexities such as innovation, technology, and dynamic market competition in the growth of potential firms to global marketplace. For example, previous observations in various research studies reveal that four factors that drove Japanese firms' early export growth include strong corporate models and cultures, a domestic market isolated from competition, an agreeable labor force, and a cohesive, homogenous leadership. But when the firms moved into foreign markets, those strengths became downfalls. Entrenched in their corporate ways, they were too narrow-minded to look for local insights, and they lacked leaders who had international knowledge. They were also unprepared for contentious overseas labor relations and the sophistication and expertise of their global competitors. Thus, to avoid Japan's fate, emerging giants must change their business models, reduce their reliance on protected domestic markets, learn to cope with diverse labor, and shake up their leadership (Black and Morrison 2010).

Focus Group Administration

Focus group is a specially invited forum that reviews the scope of research, and participants express their views with circular reasoning.[1] A focus group shares many common features with less structured interviews. Commonly, a focus group may be understood as a group discussion on a particular topic organized for research purposes. This discussion is monitored and recorded, and sometimes guided by a researcher called a moderator or facilitator. Focus groups, originating in the 1940s in the work of the Bureau of Applied Social Research at Columbia University, were first used in market research. Eventually the success of focus groups as a marketing tool in the private sector resulted in its use in public sector marketing, such as in the assessment of the impact of health education campaigns. However, focus group techniques, as used in public and private sectors, have diverged over time.

Focus group studies can be conducted by inviting some respondents who are knowledgeable in the subject of research and can share their unbiased opinion. The size of a focus group varies from 6 to 12 participants. The optimum size for a focus group is six to eight participants (excluding

---

[1] Circular reasoning is a logical myth in which the person begins with what he is trying to conclude. The components of a circular argument are often logically valid because if the premises are true, the conclusion must be true.

researchers). However, the ideal size of focus group to hold discussions could be eight participants. To initiate the focus group discussion, the researcher should brief the focus group about the objectives of the study, proposed research instrument, and study design. Upon setting the house for interactions, researcher should allow brainstorming among the group participants and stimulate critical analysis to explore key variables for the study. The proceedings of the focus group can be recorded in an electronic devise with the permission of group members, and the researcher should adhere to the confidentiality and ethical code of research in managing the information. Conventionally, researchers document minutes of the meeting and take out key indicators that are contextual and relevant to the study. One of the principal objectives of organizing a focus group is to explore variables of the study as expressed by the respondents and use them in developing research instrument for survey. A questionnaire developed in this way is easy to qualify in the pilot testing process and provides quality data for analysis. Group size is an important consideration in focus group research. It is advised that a researcher might slightly overinvite members than the standard quorum for a focus group, and potentially manage a slightly larger group. The rate of attendance in focus groups is sensitive to cost, time, interest, and the sitting fee. Hence, focus groups are often cancelled due to low attendance and unsatisfactory discussion. Small groups have the risk of limited discussion, while large groups can be chaotic and hard to streamline for the moderator if the discussion turns to sensitive issues like caste, religion, leaders, or political ideologies. If the focus groups are not streamlined properly, the discussions turn personal and become frustrating for participants who feel their voice has been slashed and they have not been given sufficient opportunity to speak (Rajagopal 2018).

A researcher serves as moderator in a focus group to streamline the discussion of a preselected topic. Consequently, the information leans toward the researcher-directed and publicly stated data administration systems. Therefore, focus group is considered as a compromise between the strengths of participant observation and individual interviewing. As a compromise between strengths and weaknesses of these other two qualitative techniques, focus groups are not as strong as they are within their specialized domain. Focus groups operate across traditional boundaries, and therefore researchers need to refine their observation, and streamline individual interviewing process. This flexibility would generate sustainable strength of focus groups. A researcher should inquire from the participants about their knowledge and experience on the topic of research to verify the appropriateness of the focus group. With participants having poor knowledge on the topic, the focus group research cannot be built to backup data collection strategies and integrated in the research design.

The composition of a focus group can be homogeneous or heterogeneous. A researcher needs to take meticulous care to get the best quality of discussion. It is advised that for a research study evaluating a community program, constitution of a homogeneous group comprising the beneficiaries of the program would be appropriate. On the other hand, for research on innovation and technology, a heterogeneous focus group comprising innovators, technocrats, market players, consumers, and regulators would be the right choice. However, there is no single approach to group composition, and group-mix will always have an impact on the data. A significant parameter in constituting the focus group is to ensure quality interaction, valid information, and noncontroversial discussion during the session. Effective interaction is key to a successful focus group, which means that a preexisting group might interact best for research purposes. A researcher should observe both controlled and noncontrolled group interactions during the variable selection process. Preexisting groups may be easier to recruit, have shared experiences, and enjoy a comfort and familiarity, which facilitates discussion or the ability to challenge each other comfortably. In health settings, preexisting groups can overcome the issues relating to disclosure of potentially stigmatizing status, which people may find uncomfortable in stranger groups. In other research projects, it may be decided that noncontrol groups are able to speak more freely without the fear of repercussion, and challenges to other participants may be more probing, leading to richer data.

In view of the strengths of focus groups, qualitative inquiries in the groups serve as the best source to produce an opportunity to conduct longitudinal and wider geo-demographic research on the topic. This combination enables researchers to learn about the participant in detail and arrange the observations systematically to support the content analysis of individual interviews. Focus groups are more controlled than liberal participation and observation forums, as the researcher defines the discussion topics in the focus groups. However, as the participants widely define the nature of group interaction, the focus group setting often turns less controlled than individual interviewing, unless there is a systematic stage-gate process to conduct the focus group research. Focus groups are created and directed by the researchers on a specific topic. Accordingly, the groups make the information flow distinctly less naturalistic than participant observation. Therefore, there is always some residual uncertainty about the accuracy of what the participants say. However, there is a significant concern that the moderator, in the name of maintaining the interview's focus, may influence the group's interactions. This problem is very common in the focus groups because the researcher influences the data collection process in most social science research studies.

Anthropomorphic Research Studies

Qualitative research methodology is an appropriate design to study anthropomorphic expressions of the subjects in the areas of sociocultural, ethnic, political, and consumption patterns. Most consumers exhibit satisfaction as a materialistic perception instead of deriving perceptual value based on self-congruity, motivations, and consumption experience derived through consumer relationships. Conventionally, consumers tend to be more responsible in acquiring comprehensive information about brands for making buying decisions in reference to perceived satisfaction and societal values (Giesler and Veresiu 2014). Consumer expectations are portrayed for self-image revelation, which play a major role in making buying decisions and determining consumer behavior. Vogue brands are generally positioned as high-end products. They motivate middle- and upper-class consumers for experimentation and develop a social pattern-based consumption spread across spatial and temporal dimension. Self-congruity theory explains that the congruence resulting from a cognitive comparison involving the product, user image, and the self-concept of consumers, affects the consumer behavior. Self-congruence leads to satisfaction by developing consumer values in reference to the attributes of products and services comprising referred experience, image, and brand reputation. Millennial consumers develop self-congruence on brands in view of the peer culture, and contemporary social values. Peer motivation drives them to assimilate to their social group by conforming on identity-signaling attributes such as premium brands, uniqueness attributes such as color, and the price-affordability ratio (Chan et al. 2012; Gofman et al. 2010).

Self-image congruence analyzes the cognitive dimensions of attention (self and social), interest, desire, and derived satisfaction that develop preferences for brands among millennial consumers. Self-image congruence affects positive attitudes toward brands built through advertising effectiveness, market and social influence on consumer preferences, peer attitude, perceived quality, and brand preferences. Self-image congruence is related to the self-concept of the consumer and the social significance of vogue brands that determine the market trends. Millennial consumers, therefore, prefer vogue brands to boost their ideal social self-concept. A positive relationship between self-image congruence and the high-end vogue brands develops consumer preferences toward buying and getting associated with such brands in the long run (Rhee and Johnson 2012). The relationship between self-image congruence and cognitive variables, such as consumption experience, satisfaction, and brand value, affects consumer behavior. Self-concept describes individuals' ideas and perceptions concerning a brand. The self-concept includes perceived abilities public image, and personality. Consumers express their self-image through brand personality, which attributes to emotions, and perceived satisfaction of fashion brands. Therefore, brand manifestation plays key role in driving consumer cognition toward trendy and unfamiliar brands.

Qualitative Loop Analysis

In longitudinal qualitative research, information loops are often generated due to repetition in interview questions and related responses at different space and time environments. Information loops occur during information acquisition process due to unclear presentation of questions to subjects. Research instruments, which consist of unstructured and semistructured questions, often trigger loops in qualitative inquiries as they lead to ambiguous responses and fuzzy interpretations to overlapping contents. The focus group and participatory research methods also tend to generate qualitative loops, as they are often unstructured and controlled by the subjects. Sometimes, as the focus of the research shifts over spatial and temporal dimensions, the core and peripheral variables, which are key to information acquisition, change, resulting into loop in the perceptions and expressions of respondents. Information loops deliver unclear responses, which are disjointed to earlier viewpoints. Therefore, information loops in qualitative research need to be carefully analyzed by applying necessary information filters to complete set of information or in partial segments. The critical responses need to be analyzed in reference to causes and effects, self-image congruence of the subjects in context of the questions asked, and their psychosocial perspectives. The critical analysis of contents would help researcher in breaking the loop and rationally examining the responses. The researchers should minimize intercept questions and determine their need by evaluating the quality of responses shared by the subjects. The nonconventional wisdom suggests that the researchers should smoothen the qualitative research loop by developing intercept questions as inductive, response-induced, disruptive, or as a radical requirement to seek refined information from the subjects. However, seeking feedback from the subjects on the researcher's observation and fast-track information analysis also open the loop for extended qualitative inquiries. In the feedback sessions, subjects generally reinforce value to the statements, though some may change the opinion. The principal factors affecting the qualitative inquiry loop are shown in Figure 4.2.

Loops in qualitative research are formed when the research focus is changed over time due to sociopolitical changes and ideological shifts in a longitudinal research. Feedback loop analysis, simply referred as loop analysis, is a method that applies qualitative models to dynamic systems. It allows representing the dimensions of research and interactions between variables. The study interactions to predict the response of the subjects by modifying the core and peripheral variables in qualitative inquiry is called perturbation. The loop analysis method is frequently applied in ecology and social development and is currently used for exploring associations of consumers between cognitive variables related to consumption pattern and behavioral trends in the marketplace.

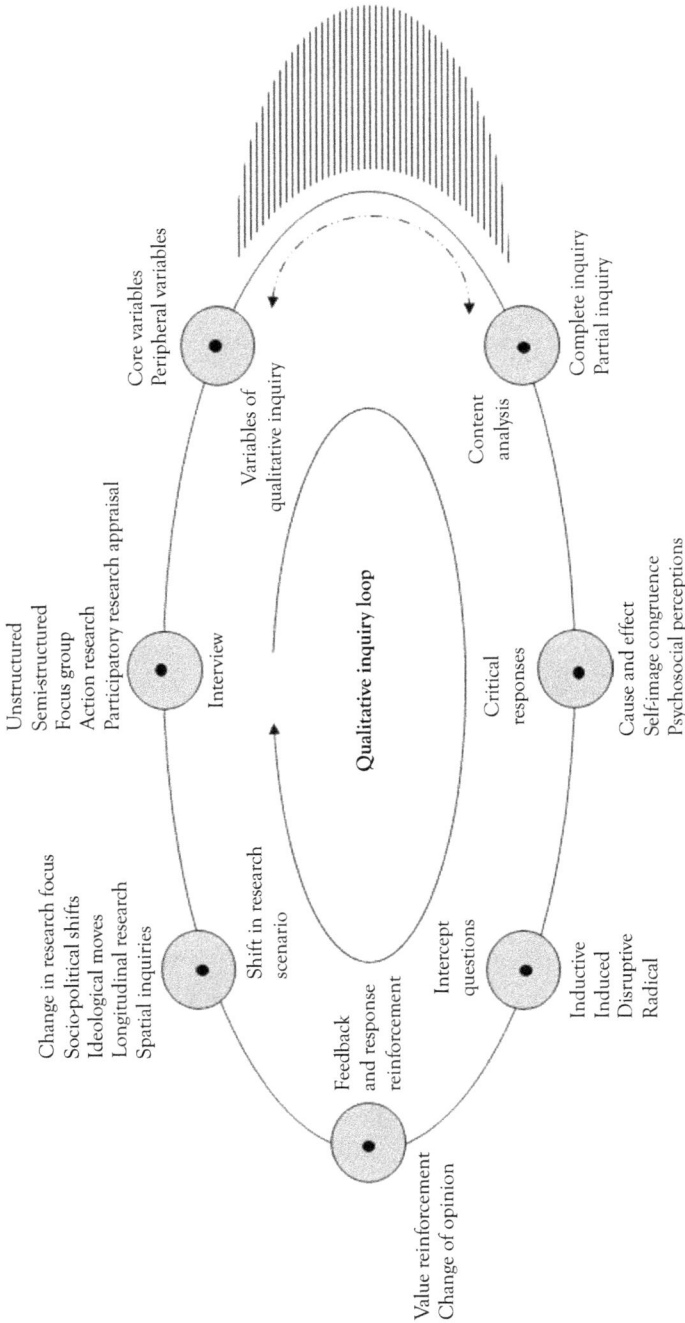

Figure 4.2 Qualitative inquiry loop: concepts and path

Reasoned Action and Differentiation Strategy

Theory of reasoned action (TRA) may be explained in context to the consumer choices under market competition, in which consumer behavior is determined by the intention to lean toward a choice of product and service and develops norms of association with it. Intention to choose a product or service is the cognitive representation of a consumer's readiness to explore satisfaction and derive comparative use values and value for money. Consumer's intention to buy products and services is determined by their specific perceptions on gaining value through comparative advantages, and perceived behavioral control. Supplementing to the variables of consumers' purchase intentions behavior, theory of planned behavior argues that attitudes of consumers derived by the social media and peer influences help in fostering their preferences on products and services in competitive markets. Majority of companies engage market research agencies to monitor and measure the dynamics of consumer attitudes that are governed by continuously updating their knowledge, changing beliefs, and social interactions. The perceived behavioral control of consumers also influences intentions.

Theory of planned behavior (TPB) emerged in the late twentieth century as an outgrowth of TRA and has been used successfully to predict and explain a wide range of organizational behavior of business companies in the global marketplace. Most companies growing amidst market competition drive their efforts to change the purchase intentions of consumers in their favor to gain sustainable advantage over the competition and inject butterfly effect in the market. The TPB states that the consumer behavior is largely driven by motivation, which develops intention, while behavioral control demonstrates the ability of consumers to turn buying intentions into action. Such planned behavior and reasoned action distinguishes between beliefs, normative behavior, and behavioral control. The TPB exhibits the following constructs that collectively represent the analytical insights and carry out dynamic expulsion of small changes for large difference that explains the butterfly effect:

- Attitudes: This refers to the critical evaluation of purchase intentions and expected benefits of the buying behavior of consumers. It entails a consideration of the outcomes of right buying decision.

- Behavioral intention: This exhibits the motivational factors that influence a given behavior, which demonstrates that the stronger the purchase intention, the more sustainable the consumer behavior.
- Subjective norms: This refers to the opinion whether most consumers approve or disapprove of the behavior and seek second opinion from the peers or look for public outlook. It relates to consumers' opinion whether peers guide the personal insights toward decision-making.
- Social norms: This refers to the social code of behavior in a group of people or larger cultural settings. Social norms, which most consumers set as their decision-making benchmark, are considered normative, or standard, in a group of people.
- Perceived power: This refers to the consumers' bargaining power and perceived value analysis on the decisions that may facilitate or impede the judgmental behavior of consumers. Perceived power contributes to a consumer's perceived behavior also in reference to the competitive products.

Some studies counterargue cognitive intricacies between behavioral intention and actual behavior in determining consumer preferences and giving a lead to the brand in the marketplace. Perceived behavioral control analysis also helps companies in predicting behavioral intention and probable shifts in the consumer behavior. In addition, consumers are also driven by social cognitive elements such as motivation and performance, and feelings of frustration associated with repeated failures that determine effect and behavioral reactions. In a competitive marketplace, where determining the comparative advantages are complex, the consumer behavior is largely determined by self-efficacy and value expectancy parameters. Self-efficacy may be defined as the conviction emerging from ACCA model (Rajagopal 2011) comprising accessibility to products, comprehension, conviction, and action. Self-efficacy attitude successfully executes the behavior required to produce the desired values. The value expectancy refers to a consumers' estimation about the degree of satisfaction that will lead to certain outcomes. The self-efficacy is the most important precondition for behavioral change, since it has the potential to induce the community behavior.

Summary

Many qualitative studies are founded on inductive theories, which allow the researcher to generate research propositions from analyzing the initial round of collected data. The questions supporting the research propositions are the distinguishing factors between qualitative and quantitative research. Therefore, qualitative data analysis is often challenged, as it is not a stand-alone methodological approach to the opinion analysis of subjects on various social, anthropological, ethnographic, and cognitive studies. Narrative analysis supported by the imagery or documented evidence would be able to authenticate the results and the possibility of its generalization. Consequently, evidence-based research has become prominent in qualitative research. The research-based practice programs like social laboratories, action research programs, and community health care system provide a systematic, participative approach to the design, implementation, and evaluation of evidence-based practice guidelines for the qualitative researchers to evaluate its causes and effects. Evidence-based qualitative research process helps in mapping consumer perceptions, emotions, attitudes, and behavior across time and geo-demographic segments.

Another dimension in evidence-based qualitative research has emerged as action research over time. Confirmatory study design exhibits how the subjects interpret their behavior in a study environment. The action research projects developed and implemented in social and ethnological perspectives are commonly defined as social development projects driven on the human elements. As action research is derived from the qualitative research design, it is implemented using a participatory methodology by involving subjects and role players in a research project. In action research projects, participants are constituted in teams with allocation of tasks within the predetermined research domains.

Participatory research appraisal (PRA) has evolved over time, within the broad context of evidence-based research, as a qualitative approach to plan community research projects. This approach is based on voluntary participation of subjects to document their knowledge and opinions in planning social and business development projects and programs. PRA engages the total population, irrespective of a defined sample size to develop concept maps and action research plans. PRA methodology has been widely used to explore business opportunities in the rural or bottom-of-the-pyramid geo-demographic segments. The participatory research has been useful in exploring the ways in which businesses use and create diverse forms of rural and social capital.

Researchers in view of managing information from small samples have further fragmented the qualitative research designs into convenience samples. Evidence-based research is usually conduced within a small, representative sample population. Case research has emerged as an extended dimension of qualitative research in the recent past to put forth evidence derived from narrow samples for wider discussions and interpretations. It is a narrative analysis of a given social or business related problem explained with a protagonist. A business case study is essentially a story about a problem, challenge, or opportunity faced by a manager or stakeholders. A case research can be conducted using qualitative tools and techniques. Case research is popularly used in ethnographic studies as the major research methodology to explore the problems associated with the human elements in society, business and governance.

A focus group shares many common features with less structured interviews. Commonly, a focus group may be understood as a group discussion on a particular topic organized for research purposes. Focus groups are monitored and recorded, and sometimes guided by a researcher called a moderator or facilitator. The focus group and participatory approaches are useful exercises for exploratory marketing research. However, small groups have the risk of having limited discussion, while large groups can be chaotic and hard to streamline for the moderator if the discussion turns to sensitive issues like caste, religion, leaders, or political ideologies.

The focus groups serve as the best source to conduct the longitudinal studies.

This chapter argues that in longitudinal qualitative research, often information loops are generated due to repetition in interview questions and related responses at different space and time environments. The information loops during the information acquisition process occur due to unclear presentation of questions to subjects. The loops in qualitative research are formed when research focus is changes over time due to socio-political changes and ideological shifts in a longitudinal research. Feedback loop analysis, referred to simply as loop analysis is a method that applies qualitative models to dynamic systems.

References

Andersson, C., and P. Runeson. 2007. "A Spiral Process Model for Case Studies on Software Quality Monitoring Method and Metrics." *Software Process Improving Practice* 12, no. 2, pp. 125–40.

Avison, D., F. Lau, M. Myers, and P.A. Nielsen. 1999. "Action Research." *Communications of the ACM* 42, no. 1, pp. 94–97.

Baxter, P., and S. Jack. 2008. "Qualitative Case Study Methodology: Study Design and Implementation for Novice Researchers." *The Qualitative Report* 13, no. 4, pp. 544–59.

Benbasat, I., D.K. Goldstein, and M. Mead. 1987. "The Case Research Strategy in Studies of Information Systems." *MIS Quarterly* 11, no. 3, pp. 369–86.

Black, N. 1994. "Why We Need Qualitative Research." *Journal of Epidemiology and Community Health* 48, no. 5, pp. 425–26.

Bosworth, G., and R. Turner. 2018. "Interrogating the Meaning of a Rural Business Through a Rural Capitals Framework." *Journal of Rural Studies* 60, no. 1, pp. 1–10.

Burck, C. 2005. "Comparing Qualitative Research Methodologies for Systemic Research: The Use of Grounded Theory, Discourse Analysis and Narrative Analysis." *Journal of Family Therapy* 27, no. 3, pp. 237–62.

Brydon-Miller, M., D. Greenwood, and P. Maguire. 2003. "Why Action Research?" *Action Research* 1, no. 1, pp. 9–28.

Chambers, R. 1994. "The Origins and Practice of Participatory Rural Appraisal." *World Development* 22, no. 7, pp. 953–69.

Chan, C., J. Berger, and L. Boven. 2012. "Identifiable But Not Identical: Combining Social Identity and Uniqueness Motives in Choice." *Journal of Consumer Research* 39, no. 3, pp. 561–73.

Dalton, J., A. Booth, J. Noyes, and A.J. Sowden. 2017. "Potential Value of Systematic Reviews of Qualitative Evidence in Informing User-centered Health and Social Care: Findings from a Descriptive Overview." *Journal of Clinical Epidemiology* 88, no. 1, pp. 37–46.

Eden, C., and F. Ackermann. 2018. "Theory into Practice, Practice to Theory: Action Research in Method Development." *European Journal of Operational Research* 27, no. 3, pp. 1145–55.

Farber, N.K. 2006. "Conducting Qualitative Research: A Practical Guide for School Counselors." *Professional School Counseling* 9, no. 5, pp. 367–75.

Flyvbjerg, B. 2006. "Five Misunderstandings about Case-study Research." *Qualitative Inquiry* 12, no. 2, pp. 219–45.

Giesler, M., and E. Veresiu. 2014. "Creating the Responsible Consumer: Moralistic Governance Regimes and Consumer Subjectivity." *Journal of Consumer Research* 41, no. 3, pp. 840–57.

Gofman, A., H.R. Moskowitz, M. Bevolo, and T. Mets. 2010. "Decoding Consumer Perceptions of Premium Products with Rule-developing Experimentation." *Journal of Consumer Marketing* 27, no. 5, pp. 425–36.

Green, J., K. Willis, E. Hughes, R. Small, N. Welch, L. Gibbs, and J. Daly. 2007. "Generating Best Evidence from Qualitative Research: The Role of Data Analysis." *Australian and New Zealand Journal of Public Health* 31, no. 6, pp. 545–50.

Hickey, S.D., S.J. Maidment, K.M. Heinemann, Y.L. Roe, and S.V. Kildea. 2018. "Participatory Action Research Opens Doors: Mentoring Indigenous Researchers to Improve Midwifery in Urban Australia." *Women and Birth* 31, no. 4, pp. 263–68.

Magids, S., A. Zorfas, and D. Leemon. 2015. "New Science of Consumer Emotions." *Harvard Business Review* 93, no. 11, pp. 68–77.

Menconi, M.E., D. Grohmann, and C. Mancinelli. 2017. "European Farmers and Participatory Rural Appraisal: A Systematic Literature Review on Experiences to Optimize Rural Development." *Land Use Policy* 60, no. 1, pp. 1–11.

Ohman, A. 2005. "Qualitative Methodology for Rehabilitation Research." *Journal of Rehabilitation Medicine* 37, no. 5, pp. 273–80.

Popay, J., and G. Williams. 1998. "Qualitative Research and Evidence-based Healthcare." *Journal of the Royal Society of Medicine* 91, no. Suppl. 35, pp. 32–37.

Rajagopal, A. 2011. "Impact of Radio Advertisements on Buying Behaviour of Urban Commuters." *International Journal of Retail and Distribution Management* 39, no. 7, pp. 480–503.

Rajagopal, A. 2018. *Marketing Research: Fundamentals, Process, and Implications.* Hauppauge, New York, NY: Nova Publishers.

Reason, P., and H. Bradbury. 2001. *Handbook of Action Research*. London, UK: Sage Publications.

Rhee, J., and K.K.P. Johnson. 2012. "Investigating Relationships Between Adolescents' Liking for an Apparel Brand and Brand Self-congruence." *Young Consumers: Insight and Ideas for Responsible Marketers* 13, no. 1, pp. 74–85.

Robinson, H., J. Segal, and H. Sharp. 2007. "Ethnographically Informed Empirical Studies of Software Practice." *Information and Software Technology* 49, no. 6, pp. 540–51.

Robson, C. 2005. *Real World Research*, 5th ed. Malden, MA: Blackwell.

Runeson, P., and M. Höst. 2009. "Guidelines for Conducting and Reporting Case Study Research in Software Engineering." *Empirical Software Engineering* 14, no. 2, pp. 131–64.

Yin, R.K. 2003. "Case Study Research." *Design and Methods*, 3rd ed. London: Sage.

CHAPTER 5

Mixed Methods and Qualitative Software

Overview

Mixed method research (MMR) design has evolved over time into a contemporary paradigm to accommodate the statistical decisions and qualitative perceptions of subjects in a longitudinal and spatial research and to interpret the results objectively. MMR offers researchers an opportunity to develop inductive theories and simultaneously test the deductive theories in complex disciplines like cognitive sciences, psychometric studies, and obscure sociological studies. Evidence-based research in clinical trials of medicines and social innovation projects have widely used the MMR approaches. This chapter discusses the salient attributes of MMR and argues the benefits of integrating the qualitative and quantitative research designs in a single study. The specific data analysis method includes data mining, text analytics, business intelligence analysis, and data visualizations. Qualitative research has emerged today with an enhanced scope in business management in conjunction with the social media driven digital marketing, which is increasingly getting complex and multidimensional. In addition, the prominent quantitative data analysis techniques such as regression analysis, discriminant function analysis, factor analysis, cluster analysis, and conjoint analysis have been discussed in detail in this chapter. There are four criteria comprising implementation, priority, integration, and theoretical perspectives to choose the MMR strategy. The chapter argues that majority of longitudinal studies follow pragmatic information analysis systems using statistical software and Big Data analytics programs. There is still a wider scope for descriptive and explanatory research studies in the social science and business management areas.

Quantitative research is considered a prominent methodology in decision sciences and has been extended widely to the social sciences.

However, qualitative inquiries have been serving as evidence-based research approaches in the social science and community health research areas. Mixed research methodologies have emerged as a contemporary paradigm to accommodate the statistical decisions and perceptions of subjects in a longitudinal and spatial research to make decisions with objectivity. Qualitative and quantitative research approaches, thus, become a widely used mode of inquiry in many disciplines including sociology, anthropology, behavioral sciences, epistemology, political research, and business and management science. Depending on the choices made across spatial and temporal research dimensions, mixed-methods can provide an investigator with various design choices spanning across a range of sequential and concurrent decision metrics. The mixed research methods are used in social and health quality control measures through evidence-based clinical trials, and ethical concerns. Mixed methods researches are compatible in working with different types of data like time-series and one point of time data. It may also involve different research teams working in different research paradigms at the same time. Therefore, the mixed method research is often referred to as multi-strategy research implying the application of a number of different research methodologies addressing a complex range of research questions embedded in a complex research design. As stated earlier, mixed research methods are used in longitudinal studies pursued by a group of researchers, consecutively over time and across the geo-demographic study regions (Bryman 2001; Morse 2003). MMR offers researchers an opportunity to develop inductive theories and simultaneously test the deductive theories in complex disciplines like cognitive sciences, psychometric studies, and obscure sociological studies. Hence, MMR is regarded as a tool "outside the box" in most research areas. As this method uses both quantitative and qualitative approaches, it has the advantages of both precision and comprehension in interpreting the information.

In general, the mixed methods research offers therefore both opportunities and risks. The opportunities include exploring human elements in the research topic against the closed questions leading to the numeric values for statistical analysis. However, the risks include biases in both qualitative inquiries and quantitative analysis. Quantitative research, as a positivist paradigm, has historically been the cornerstone of social science research. However, it has always been a challenge for the researchers to eliminate their biases and remain emotionally detached during the statistical analysis of empirical data while applying quantitative data to test and justifying the hypotheses through the construct of measures. Contrary to the data analysis and interpretation in the quantitative research design, qualitative study designs pursue a constructivist or interpretivist paradigm, which contends that statistical analysis has isolated standpoints, and ignores the cognitive conjunctions in the research (Johnson and Onwuegbuzie 2004). Accordingly, it can be argued that in either qualitative or quantitative research designs:

- Generalizations are neither desirable nor possible in a time- and context-free research designs.
- Research is value bound and human element in inquiries contribute to the value.
- It is impossible to fully differentiate causes and effects, and interpret the quantitative results.
- Logic flows from specific to general and vice versa in both the qualitative and quantitative research, but bias prevails in both study designs.
- Subjects and researcher cannot be separated because the information revelation by the subject is the only source of reality in both methodologies.

Researchers have expressed in many studies that the MMR is compatible with conducting studies with structured and semistructured interviews in various disciplines of social and health sciences. Evidence-based research in clinical trials of medicines and social innovation projects have widely used the MMR approaches. Many social scientists believe today that there are larger number of research areas where the mixed method research appears to be appropriate. The emerging disciplines that use mixed research study designs include nursing, psychology, marketing, education, library and information science, information systems, and health care management.

Ethnographic research meticulously employs qualitative research methodologies using the grounded theory paradigm and also administers the quantitative data on independent variables systematically. Such blend of dual research methodologies generates continuous interplay between analysis and data collection to quantify changes in cognitive elements of the subjects. In MMR, the inductive and deductive analytics are used to derive the applied perspectives (grounded theory) and test the existing theories (deductive methodology) in the context of research. Qualitative research is concerned with finding the explorative responses by asking the subjects fundamental questions such as why, what, where, when, which, and who embedded within the research instrument. Contrary to the prior pattern of inquiry, quantitative research focuses more on measuring the frequency and trend of variables responsible for cause and effects. The principal features of MMR can be discussed in view of the following attributes of this methodology:

- Qualitative research documents opinions, experiences, and feelings of individuals through narrations, storyboards, and subjective propositions.
- Qualitative research describes social phenomena, cognitive evolution of thoughts and perceptions, and naturally occurrence of responses to the directly posed questions.
- Qualitative research is ethically bound, which rules out the adjustment of data unlike in the experimental quantitative research.
- Quantitative research depends on the predetermined research models and its contextual dependent and independent variables, while the qualitative research gains understanding of the ecosystem of subjects through a holistic perspective.
- Inductive approach is employed in qualitative research to develop theory in context to the research problem, while the quantitative research is deductive and engaged in testing theories that have already been proposed in the previous research studies.
- Qualitative data are collected direct from the subjects using appropriate inquiry approaches such as in-depth interviews, focus groups, participatory approaches, and observations.

- The sampling techniques used the quantitative research are as complex as probability proportion sampling, and are large and categorical unlike the small and convenience samples in the quantitative research. Qualitative sampling techniques are concerned with seeking information within the group taxonomies and small geo-demographic populations.

Qualitative research practices are growing parallel to the quantitative research applications, as the market today has been largely influenced by the intangible variables, which could be better researched through the in-depth inquiries. Consumer behavior is continuously changing, and social media is playing a critical role in determining marketing decisions. The research in the areas of consumer behavior, grapevine effect of social media, and organizational culture can be well studied through qualitative research techniques. Qualitative research has emerged today with an enhanced scope in business management in conjunction with the social media driven digital marketing, which is increasingly getting complex and multidimensional. The strength of qualitative research has been evidenced in understanding context and interrelationships of cognitive human factors with decision sciences in business and management. It continues to represent a broad and prevalent set of challenges extended beyond business research to political, economic, and social domains. Qualitative research faces some challenges like quantitative research techniques in terms of validation and generalization of research findings. Qualitative research, therefore, has an increasing potential to determine the human involvement in business and related disciplines. Managers face some major challenges in accepting the findings of qualitative research, as these are heterogeneous and descriptive in nature. The hidden challenge with the qualitative research is to conduct it in a scientific manner and to validate the findings. It requires a highly active engagement from the researchers, respondents, and managers to conduct qualitative research scientifically, and needs great deal of effort to encapsulate intellectual, practical, physical, and emotional information analytics (Rajagopal 2018).

Despite a streamlined qualitative research methodology, the organization of business research, writing styles, language, canvasing the discussion, presenting arguments, and focusing the core features of syntheses varies widely according to the schools of thought. For example, an enormous literature needs to be reviewed to understand the debate on qualitative research perspectives among classical, neo-classical, modern, and liberal schools of thoughts.

Quantitative Methods

Data from any source in the raw form need to be adjusted to fit into the analytical design of the study. The process of evaluating data using analytical and logical reasoning is carried out to examine each component of the data provided. Data analysis is a vast exercise, not confined to just one method. Data need to be validated, and analytical technique needs to be determined based on the nature and quality of data and the objectives of the study. The data analytics plan need to be determined while conducting a research experiment. In this process, data collected from various sources is reviewed, validated, and then analyzed to exhibit results for interpretation and conclusion. Specific data analysis method includes data mining, text analytics, business intelligence analysis, and data visualizations. There are different procedures for data analysis to extract information from a given data set, as given in the following.

Regression Analysis

Regression analysis is a statistical tool for investigation of the relationships between the dependent and independent variables. Usually, a researcher seeks to ascertain the cause and effect of one variable upon another, like the effect of a promotion of product and service on its demand, or the effect of changes in the money supply on the rate of inflation in a country and commodity prices. To explore such issues, a researcher can prepare the set of underlying variables representing independency in relation to a single dependent variable and employ regression analysis to estimate the quantitative effect of the causal variables upon the variables they influence. The investigator also typically assesses the statistical significance test of the estimated relationships, which explains that the derived relationship among variables is close to the estimated relationship, and indicates the degree of confidence.

Regression analysis is used to identify the trend using a time series data of one or more variables. A researcher distinguishes the variables as dependent and independent in nature. The analysis highlights the contribution of variables to variations in the dependent variable. The analysis, if carried by two or more independent variables, is termed as multiple regressions. One prerequisite for such analysis is a time-series data of the variables identified. Regression analysis is a statistical process of estimating the relationships among variables, which includes techniques for modeling and analyzing several variables with focus on the relationship between a dependent variable and one or more independent variables. The assumptions in regression analysis include number of cases, accuracy of data, missing data, outliers, normality, linearity, homoscedasticity,[1] multi co-linearity and singularity effects of data sets. An outlier in statistics is generally observed either due to variability in the measurement, or an experimental error. The latter is sometimes excluded from the data set. The two primary uses for regression in business are forecasting and optimization. In addition to helping managers predict such things as future demand for their products, regression analysis helps fine-tune manufacturing and delivery processes. The simple regression equation can be set as:

$$Y = \propto + \beta X \qquad \qquad \text{(i)}$$

where Y indicates dependent variable and X denotes independent variable. This relationship can be measured with the coefficient β. In the previous equation $\propto$ is constant. Contrary to the simple regression analysis, multiple regression is a technique that allows additional factors to enter the analysis separately so that the effect of each can be estimated. It is valuable for quantifying the impact of various simultaneous influences upon a single dependent variable. However, because of omitted variables bias with simple regression, multiple regression is often essential even when

---

[1] Homoscedasticity describes a situation in which the error term or random variation in the relationship between the independent variables and the dependent variable is the same across all values of the independent variables.

the investigator is only interested in the effects of one of the independent variables. The equation for measuring the multiple regression is as illustrated as follows:

$$Y = \alpha + \beta_1 x_1 + \beta_2 x_2 + \cdots + \varepsilon \qquad \text{(ii)}$$

In the preceding equation, Y indicates dependent variable and $x_1, x_2 \ldots$ denote independent variables. This relationship on independent variables to dependent variable is measured with the coefficients $\beta_1, \beta_2 \ldots$ In the previously shown equation α is constant and ε represents error term.

The magnitude and direction of independent variables are determined by the slope parameter $\beta_1, \beta_2 \ldots$, and the status of the dependent variable when the independent variable is absent is given by the intercept parameter β_0. An error term ε captures the amount of variation not predicted by the slope and intercept terms. The regression coefficient (R^2) shows how well the values fit the data. Regression thus shows us how variation in one variable co-occurs with variation in another. What regression cannot show is causation; causation is only demonstrated analytically, through substantive theory.

As the competition is increasing continuously and market management process is becoming complex, dependency on statistical tools to drive precision in developing marketing strategies is growing. The most common use of regression in business is observed toward forecasting the demand, consumer behavior, price response, and market share of the company. Demand analysis, for example, predicts the number of units of a product that consumers will purchase. Many other key parameters other than demand are the dependent variables in regression models. Predicting the number of shoppers, who will pass in front of a particular billboard or Internet advertisement, may help company assess the outreach and frequency of viewing of the advertisement, and how much to pay for an advertisement. Insurance companies heavily rely on regression analysis to estimate how many policy holders would make the accident claims or turn as victims of automobile robbery, for example.

Discriminant Function Analysis

Discriminant function analysis is used to classify subjects (respondents) into predetermined groups. It is a multivariate analogue of analysis of variance, and can be considered as a posterior procedure of multivari-ate analysis of variance. This method is used to determine the impact of particular variables(s) on the dependent variable. This statistical process helps in finding the discriminating variables that could be combined in a forecasting equation to lead better for the group cluster. This analysis is being used to identify and develop criteria for market segmentation, and also to examine consumer behavior with reference to brand choice. Discriminant function is a statistical analysis used to predict a categorical dependent variable called grouping variable, by one or more continuous or binary independent variables known as predictor variables. Discrimi-nant function analysis is used to determine which continuous variables discriminate between two or more naturally occurring groups. For exam-ple, a company wants to investigate which variables discriminate between consumer of dental care products by young consumers, elderly consum-ers, and children. For that purpose, the company could collect data on numerous attributes of consumer preference like quality, price, need, peer influence, and sense of oral hygiene from the consumers. Most dental care products will naturally be preferred by the earlier category of consumers. Discriminant analysis could then be used to determine which variables are the best predictors of which dental care product, likely to be used by the consumers of different age groups.

The key assumption of canonical discriminant analysis is that sub-jects and variables can be assigned to only one group in advance, through some means external to the data being analyzed. Discriminant function (DA) analysis is used to determine which continuous variables discrim-inate between two or more naturally occurring groups. For example, a researcher may want to investigate which variables discriminate between breakfast cereals preferred by (1) young consumers, (2) children, or (3) elderly consumers older than 60 years. For that purpose, the researcher could collect data on numerous breakfast cereal brands consumed by each consumer groups. Most cereal brands will naturally fall into one of the three categories of consumers. Discriminant analysis could then be used to determine which variables are the best predictors of whether break-fast cereals will be eaten by consumers of different age groups. Discrim-inant function analysis is multivariate analysis of variance (MANOVA) reversed. In MANOVA, the independent variables are the groups and the dependent variables are the predictors. In DA, the independent variables are the predictors and the dependent variables are the groups. As previously mentioned, DA is generally used to predict membership in naturally occurring groups. Usually, several variables are included in a study to see which ones contribute to the discrimination between groups.

Discriminant function analysis is broken into a two-step process that includes testing the significance of a set of discriminant functions, and classification of variables. The first step is computationally identical to MANOVA. There is a matrix of total variances and co-variances; likewise, there is a matrix of pooled within-group variances and co-variances. The two matrices are compared via multivariate F tests to determine whether or not there are any significant differences with regards to all variables between groups. It is advised that the researcher should first perform the multivariate test, and, if the result is statistically significant, proceed to see which of the variables have significantly different means across the groups. Once the group means are found to be statistically significant, classification of variables is undertaken. DA automatically determines some optimal combination of variables so that the first function provides the most overall discrimination between groups, the second provides second most, and so on. Subjects are classified in the groups in which they had the highest classification scores. The maximum number of discriminant functions will be equal to the degrees of freedom, or the number of variables in the analysis, whichever is smaller.

Standardized β coefficients for each variable are determined for each significant function. The larger the standardized β coefficient, the larger is the respective variable's unique contribution to the discrimination specified by the respective discriminant function. To identify which independent variables causes discrimination between dependent variables, one can also examine the factor structure matrix with correlations between the variables and the discriminant functions. Finally, means for the significant discriminant functions are examined in order to determine between which groups the respective functions seem to discriminate (Klecka 1980).

Factor Analysis

The broad purpose of factor analysis is to encapsulate data so that the relationships among critical variables and interactive patterns among variables can be easily interpreted and understood. It is normally used to group variables into a limited set of clusters based on shared variance. Hence, it helps to isolate constructs and concepts. Factor analysis uses mathematical procedures for simplification of interrelated measures to discover patterns in a set of variables. Factor analysis essentially aims at attempting to discover the simplest method of interpretation of observed data known as parsimony. Factor analysis is used in many fields such as behavioral and social sciences, medicine, economics, and geography as a result of the technological advancements of computers (Yong and Pearce 2013). The approaches discussed earlier tend to give biased results on dependent variables due to high inter-correlations among the explanatory variables.

Factor analysis attempts to provide an explanation for the correlations of a larger set of variables. This analysis may be useful to determine the attitudes of customers toward the products of a company in a given situation. Factor analysis is a statistical method used to describe variability among observed, correlated variables in terms of a potentially lower number of unobserved variables called factors. The principal factor analysis techniques include exploratory factor analysis (EFA) and confirmatory factor analysis (CFA). CFA attempts to confirm hypotheses and uses path analysis diagrams to represent variables and factors, whereas EFA tries to uncover complex patterns by exploring the dataset and testing predictions (Child 2006). Factor analysis operates on the concept that the measurable and observable variables can be reduced to fewer discreet variables that share a common variance and are latent, which is known as reducing dimensionality (Bartholomew et al. 2011). Factor analysis is useful for studies that involve a few or hundreds of variables, and items from large questionnaires that need to be reduces to small data sets. This method is a statistical method used to study the dimensionality of a set of variables. In factor analysis, latent variables represent unobserved constructs and are referred to as factors or dimensions. The main applications of factor analysis techniques are to reduce the number of variables, and to detect structure in the relationships between variables. Therefore, factor analysis is applied as a data reduction or structure detection method. Factor analysis is used to identify latent constructs or factors. It is commonly used to reduce variables into a smaller set to save time and facilitate easier interpretations. There are many extraction techniques such as principal axis factor and maximum likelihood. Factor analysis is mathematically complex, and the criteria used to determine the number and significance of factors are vast. Interpretation of factor analysis is based on rotated factor loadings, rotated eigenvalues, and scree test. In reality, researchers often use more than one extraction and rotation technique based on pragmatic reasoning rather than theoretical reasoning (Yong and Pearce 2013).

Cluster Analysis

This process is helpful in obtaining segregated results for a group of variables of homogeneous nature. In marketing research, it is essential to set subgroups such as consumer goods, capital goods, geo-demographic variables, income levels, and the like. Analysis is done keeping in view the clustered data as one segment or factor in the statistical process. Cluster analysis is a major technique for classifying large information into manageable meaningful piles. It is a data reduction tool to create subgroups, which can be better managed than generic datasets. Clustering supermarket products based on the analysis of purchasing patterns can be used for planning store layouts to maximize spontaneous purchasing opportunities. Banking institutions use hierarchical cluster analysis to develop a typology of customers to retain the loyalty of customers. They do so by designing the best possible new financial products to meet the needs of different groups (clusters) for new product opportunities. Cluster analysis also supports the bankers' decision to match the type of product, customer segments, and the right strategy for market penetration. Brand image analysis by customer perceptions, which allows a company to see how its products are positioned in the market relative to those of its competitors, can be measured using cluster analysis. This type of analysis would be valuable for branding new products or identifying possible gaps in the market.

Conjoint Analysis

This method is used to explore the possibilities of designing and launching a new product that can attract customers. Customers are asked to rank some hypothetical products, this information is put through composite indexing, and the final ranks are computed. This method is commonly used for psychometric tests and measurements in determining behavior. It is a popular approach for ranking the performance of the product and the company in the market. These analytical approaches support the study of identifying factors, variable correlations, and interdependence in a given situation. Models help the marketing manager to come to an appropriate decision based on the logical interpretation of analytical results.

Link between the dependent variable and its determinants is specified in microdynamic statistics model. This model can be useful to explain the impact of product promotion activities on the volume of sales by studying the links between advertising expenditure, the number of media message insertions, the level of product awareness, and usage rate, and so on. Microbehavioral model hypothetically analyzes independent variables like consumers, dealers, and so on who interact and produce a report of behavior. Queuing model provides a logical base for making such decisions in the area of spatial and temporal marketing. This model is used to analyze the product-pace effect whether to make the customer wait for the product or to alter the marketing policy in view of competitive threats. This model can be effectively used in supermarkets, transport organizations, and so on. Decision-making models consist of mathematical techniques, decision theories, and the probability models, which are calculus and theory oriented. Game theory is also an important approach in the decision-making exercise. It draws attention to the identification of alternative decisions, uncertain variables and value of different results.

Approaches other than the ones discussed previously are specific to the problem. For instance, focus group analysis based on qualitative information may be done for determining product policy. It is, however, advised in the case of international marketing research, that a greater use of qualitative research techniques may be made at the initial stages of market entry. Further, a concrete research process can be developed, more complex if possible, and administered in different countries having varied social, economic, political, and legal environment.

Mixed Methodologies

Contemporary research trends show a higher inclination of researchers toward using MMR by blending the qualitative and quantitative designs in a single research study. The definition of mixed methods research used is largely based on a critical appraisal of definitions used by the researchers in various research disciplines. In this research methodology, the qualitative and quantitative viewpoints, data collection, analysis, and inference techniques are used for analyzing the narrative and numeric information across the breadth and depth of understanding and corroboration during the research process (Johnson et al. 2007). MMR is used for sequential longitudinal studies or concurrent research of one point of time. The priority to each data type is given in this method and integration of the overall data is managed systematically.

MMR has several researcher-friendly attributes that include flexibility, integration, and holistic view of the inquiry. In the MMR study design, researchers adapt to situational investigative techniques as they strive to address a range of complex questions. However, there is a need to distinguish between the two types of studies in the context of data integration and content analysis (Tashakkori and Creswell 2007). The benefits of such integration can be viewed as stated in the following:

- Flexibility in administering the research instrument
- Adding and eliminating questions
- Choosing the research methodology for a section of information collected through the research instrument
- Selecting the sequential or concurrent time for the complete study

The major challenge with MMR studies is to decide how to integrate the data, timing, and priority (Creswell and Plano Clark 2007). Thus, there is a need for guidance for conducting MMR and for assessing the rigor of data collection, and analysis of both data types. There are four criteria comprising implementation, priority, integration, and theoretical perspectives to choose MMR strategy as discussed in the following:

- MMR studies require researchers to collect both the quantitative and qualitative data in phases over time (sequentially) or that they gather it at one point of time (concurrently). When the data collection process is spread over temporal dimensions, researchers may follow either the quantitative or quantitative design of research instrument. Accordingly, a study can combine partially quantitative and qualitative data within the spatial and temporal dimensions.

- The second criteria affecting the choice of a strategy is priority or weight given to the type of data and analytics design. Researchers need to establish rationale for choosing the qualitative and quantitative attributes of the data in a MMR employed study design. The priority on study designs should be equal, or it might be skewed toward either qualitative or quantitative data. Priority for the method of data collection and analysis depends on the interests of the researcher, the audience for the study, the desired emphasis to be made in the study, and the use of a theory as an inductive or deductive framework for the study.

- In MMR study design, integration is one of the major challenges. Integration of the two types of data might occur at several stages in the process of research over the data collection, the data analysis, and interpretation phases. Integration is fundamentally blending of the data of two different study designs into one.

- The final factor to consider in MMR study is the theoretical perspective, which guides the entire design of study. The theoretical perspectives vary across the disciplines from social sciences to health sciences, and through the applied engineering research. Although all designs have implicit theories, mixed methods researchers can make the theory explicit as a guiding framework for the study.

The MMR design has received several criticisms from the mainstream researchers and theorists as it is not a consistent method of data analysis, which often exhibits biased results. MMR studies are also criticized for partially adopting the qualitative and quantitative research designs and analyzing data on the basis of assumptions (Freshwater 2007). However, mixed methods research brings different perspectives on data by combining both qualitative and quantitative analytical tools. However, researchers of MMR studies should cross-validate results to measure the accuracy.

Although the longitudinal studies are following pragmatic information analysis systems using statistical software and Big Data analytics programs, there is still a wider scope for descriptive and explanatory research studies in the social science and business management areas. By integrating quantitative and qualitative data analyses in a single study, MMR can reveal patterns of change over time, and at the same time help reveal individual and contextual factors influencing the observed patterns (Taguchi 2018).

Epistemologically, researchers still debate whether MMR supports positivist philosophy, interpretive paradigm, or pluralist schools of thought. However, regardless of whether a qualitative or quantitative method dominates, it has been argued that the foundation of MMR studies is its central premise of integrating quantitative and qualitative approaches to demonstrate better understanding of research problems (Creswell and Plano Clark 2007). Hence, through the mixing of methods, research design, analyses, interpretation, and data presentation; the values of each approach could lead to an integrated research design. The transformation of qualitative responses into numerical forms enables their analysis from quantitative perspectives (Sandelowski, Voils, and Knafl 2009; Fielding 2012). However, while quantifying the qualitative information, the major dilemma with the researcher is how to count narrations, stories, and observations. Fundamentally, the qualitatively data lack in the numerical precision with narrative complexity. Mixed methods research offers a number of conceptual, practical, and pedagogical challenges that need to be addressed if this form of inquiry is to develop its full potential in sport and exercise psychology. The MMR studies embed philosophical assumptions and the methods of inquiry (Creswell and Plano Clark 2007).

Summary

Quantitative research is considered a significant analytical design in decision sciences and has been widely applied to the social sciences also. Qualitative and quantitative research approaches, thus, become widely used modes of inquiry extended to many disciplines including sociology, anthropology, behavioral sciences, epistemology, political research, and business and management science. MMR offers researchers an opportunity to develop inductive theories and simultaneously test the deductive theories in complex disciplines. The study design of MMR is compatible in working with different types of data like time-series and one point of time data. Quantitative research has been critically examined in the chapter as a positivist paradigm, which has historically developed the foundation of social-science research. However, it has always been a challenge for the researchers to eliminate their biases, remain emotionally detached during the statistical analysis of empirical data while applying quantitative data to test, and justify the hypotheses through the construct of measures. Emerging disciplines like nursing, psychology, marketing, education, library and information science, information systems, and health care management use MMR study design. In addition, ethnographic research meticulously employs qualitative research methodologies using grounded theory paradigm and administers quantitative data on independent variables systematically.

Analyzing quantitative data is a vast exercise, which is not confined to just one method. Data need to be validated, and analytical technique needs to be determined based on the nature and quality of data and the objectives of the study. In the pretext, various prominent quantitative data analysis techniques such as regression analysis, discriminant function analysis, factor analysis, cluster analysis, and conjoint analysis have been discussed. Usually, a researcher seeks to ascertain the cause and effect of one variable upon another, like the effect of a promotion of product and service on its demand, or the effect of changes in the money supply on the rate of inflation in a country and commodity prices. To explore such analysis, a researcher sets underlying variables representing independency in relation to a single dependent variable to measure the cause and effect relationship.

Discriminant function analysis is used to classify subjects (respondents) into predetermined groups. It is a multivariate analog of analysis of variance, and can be considered as a posterior procedure of multivariate analysis of variance. This method is used to determine the impact of particular variables(s) on the dependent variable. The broad purpose of factor analysis is to encapsulate data so that the relationships among critical variables and interactive patterns among variables can be easily interpreted and understood. It is normally used to group variables into a limited set of clusters based on shared variance. The factor analysis attempts to provide an explanation for the correlations of a larger set of variables. Cluster analysis is a major technique for classifying large information into manageable meaningful piles. It is a data reduction tool to create subgroups, which can be better managed than generic datasets. The conjoint analysis method is used to explore the possibilities of designing and launching a new product that can attract customers. Customers are asked to rank some hypothetical products, this information is put through composite indexing, and the final ranks are computed. This method is commonly used for psychometric tests and measurements in determining behavior.

MMR studies have several researcher-friendly attributes that include flexibility, integration, and holistic view of the inquiry. In the MMR study design, researchers adapt to situational investigative techniques as they strive to address a range of complex questions. There are four criteria comprising implementation, priority, integration, and theoretical perspectives to choose the MMR strategy. Epistemologically, researchers still debate whether MMR supports positivist philosophy, interpretive paradigm, or pluralist schools of thought. However, regardless of whether a qualitative or quantitative method dominates, it has been argued that the MMR studies are based on its central premise of integrating quantitative and qualitative approaches to demonstrate better understanding of research problems.

References

Bryman, A. 2001. *Social Research Methods*. Oxford: Oxford University Press.

Creswell, J.W., and V.L. Plano Clark. 2007. *Designing and Conducting Mixed Methods Research*. Thousand Oaks, CA: Sage.

Fielding, N.G. 2012. "Triangulation and Mixed Methods Designs: Data Integration with New Research Technologies." *Journal of Mixed Methods Research* 6, no. 2, pp. 124–36.

Freshwater, D. 2007. "Reading Mixed Methods Research: Contexts for Criticism." *Journal of Mixed Methods Research* 1, no. 2, pp. 134–46.

Johnson, R.B., and A.J. Onwuegbuzie. 2004. "Mixed-methods Research: A Research Paradigm Whose Time Has Come." *Educational Researcher* 33, no. 7, pp. 14–26.

Johnson, R.B., A.J. Onwuegbuzie, and L.A. Turner. 2007. "Toward a Definition of Mixed-methods Research." *Journal of Mixed Methods Research* 1, no. 2, pp. 112–33.

Morse, J.M. 2003. "Principles of Mixed Method and Multi-method Research Design." In *Handbook of Mixed Methods in Social and Behavioural Research*, eds. C. Teddlie and A. Tashakkori. London, UK: Sage.

Sandelowski, M., C.I. Voils, and G. Knafl. 2009. "On Quantitizing." *Journal of Mixed Methods Research* 3, no. 3, pp. 208–22.

Taguchi, N. 2018. "Description and Explanation of Pragmatic Development: Quantitative, Qualitative, and Mixed Methods Research." *System* 75, no. 1, pp. 23–32.

Tashakkori, A., and J.W. Creswell. 2007. "Editorial: the New Era of Mixed Methods." *Journal of Mixed Methods Research* 1, no. 1, pp. 3–7.

About the Author

Rajagopal is Professor of Marketing at EGADE Business School of Monterrey Institute of Technology and Higher Education (ITESM), Mexico City Campus and Life Fellow of the Royal Society for Encouragement of Arts, Manufacture and Commerce, London. Dr. Rajagopal is also Visiting Professor at Boston University, Boston, Massachusetts. He has been listed with biography in various international directories.

He offers courses in the areas of marketing, innovation management, and international business to the students of undergraduate, graduate, and doctoral programs. He has imparted training to senior executives and has conducted over 65 management development programs to the corporate executives and international faculty. Throughout his career, Dr. Rajagopal has delivered a number of courses and executive and doctoral programs in the areas of marketing and international business in business schools including the Indian Institute of Management, at Indore and Rohtak, India; Narsee Monjee Institute of Management Studies, Mumbai, India; Institute of Public Enterprise, Hyderabad, India, and at International Management Institute, Bhubaneswar, India.

Rajagopal holds postgraduate and doctoral degrees in Economics and Marketing respectively from Ravishankar University in India. He has to his credit 55 books on marketing and innovation management themes and over 400 research contributions that include published research papers in national and international refereed journals. He is the Editor-in-Chief of *International Journal of Leisure and Tourism Marketing* and *International Journal of Business Competition and Growth*. Dr. Rajagopal is also Regional Editor of *Emerald Emerging Markets Case Studies*, published by Emerald Publishers, United Kingdom. He is on the editorial board of various journals of international repute. His research contributions have been recognized by the National Council of Science and Technology (CONACyT), Government of Mexico, by awarding him the honor of the highest level of National Researcher-SNI Level-III.

He has been awarded UK-Mexico Visiting Chair 2016–17 for collaborative research on "Global-Local Innovation Convergence" with University of Sheffield, UK, instituted by the Consortium of Higher Education Institutes of Mexico and UK.

Index

Note: page numbers followed by *f* and *t* indicates figures and tables respectively.

OTHER TITLES IN OUR MARKETING COLLECTION

Naresh Malhotra, Georgia Tech, Editor

- *Service Excellence: Creating Customer Experiences That Build Relationships* by Ruth N. Bolton
- *Relationship Marketing Re-Imagined: Marketing's Inevitable Shift from Exchanges to Value Cocreating Relationships* by Naresh K. Malhotra, Can Uslay, and Ahmet Bayraktar
- *Critical Thinking for Marketers, Volume I: Learn How to Think, Not What to Think* by Terry Grapentine, David Soorholtz, and David Dwight
- *Critical Thinking for Marketers, Volume II: Learn How to Think, Not What to Think* by Terry Grapentine, David Soorholtz, and David Dwight
- *Employee Ambassadorship: Optimizing Customer-Centric Behavior From The Inside-Out and Outside-In* by Michael W. Lowenstein
- *Social Media Marketing: Marketing Panacea or the Emperor's New Digital Clothes?* by Alan Charlesworth

Announcing the Business Expert Press Digital Library

Concise e-books business students need for classroom and research

This book can also be purchased in an e-book collection by your library as

- a one-time purchase,
- that is owned forever,
- allows for simultaneous readers,
- has no restrictions on printing, and
- can be downloaded as PDFs from within the library community.

Our digital library collections are a great solution to beat the rising cost of textbooks. E-books can be loaded into their course management systems or onto students' e-book readers.
The **Business Expert Press** digital libraries are very affordable, with no obligation to buy in future years. For more information, please visit **www.businessexpertpress.com/librarians**. To set up a trial in the United States, please email **sales@businessexpertpress.com**.

www.ingramcontent.com/pod-product-compliance
Lightning Source LLC
Chambersburg PA
CBHW061306220326
41599CB00026B/4759